31 Benning Place

KAREN LASLEY-SLIDER

First printing, 2019.

ISBN# 978-1-7338569-0-4

31 Benning Place LLC Publisher
15981 Yarnell # 119
Los Angeles, CA, 91342

www.31Benningplace.com

CONTENTS

CHAPTER 1

Ramona

31 BENNING PL.

This is a story that begins with my mother (an angel), and how she raised six kids on welfare in the worst neighborhoods in Los Angles while maintaining her core values and instilling those values in her children through stories of her childhood. Most of these stories were what my mother used to entertain us when our lights got turned off for non-payment. It wasn't a big deal to us, doing without lights or gas. We were poor, and in the neighborhood where we lived, it was a common occurrence for nearly everyone at some point.

I remember making a promise to myself at an early age that when I grew up, my kids would never go hungry. My kids would never know what it feels like to get the lights or gas cut off. I promised myself I would have a good job and enough money to pay all my bills at once. No robbing Peter to pay Paul as my mother would often call it. No living from check to check for me. My kids would never know how it feels to heat water in a crock-pot to take a hoe bath. They would never need candles to banish the darkness as the night approaches. I said to myself, "I will live in a house in a nice neighborhood with a backyard. And I will marry a good man who will support me and our five kids." I always wanted a large family. I love my brothers and sisters. We are the best of friends. All we needed to be happy was each other. I often told my mother, as I watched her struggle, "When I grow up, I will take care of you and buy you new clothes." I told her she would never have to work again. I had no idea at that age how expensive children are. Really! Five kids....

Our way of life seemed to be lacking all the bells and whistles. My cousins had so much more than we did. They lived in a house, not an apartment. My aunts and uncles had each other and worked together and built good lives for themselves. My mother was alone, doing the best she could with six little kids. It was hard for our mother to keep up; we were constantly growing and eating. It seemed like one of us always needed new shoes or new clothes. She went without so we could have what we wanted and needed. I wanted so much more for her. She cried many nights worrying about our future. She was a heavy smoker and sometimes couldn't even afford a twenty-seven-cent pack of cigarettes. We hated it when she cried, so we would run to the next-door neighbors asking for a cigarette or two.

Little did I know the impact these times would have in shaping our future! We had it harder than most growing up, but looking back, I wouldn't change a thing. I like the people we turned out to be. We learned to depend on each other and work together. The love we share would put the Waltons to shame.

We learned how to improvise and adapt, to overcome any obstacle put in our way. Our courage and determination to strive for the best in life while living in the worst neighborhoods of Los Angeles helped others around us reach for more and rise above their circumstances. It was rare for both the lights and the gas be cut off at the same time, but for a single mother, sometimes the budget just didn't stretch that far. My mother, Ramona, was a team player. She would sit us all down, show us the budget and give us a choice as to which utility we kept on. Usually we voted for the gas; we needed it for cooking and bathing, while lights were only good for watching television. Who needed to keep the refrigerator cold, considering it was always empty late in the month, except for ice cubes. When our lights were turned off, we learned to become good storytellers, and it was fun taking turns and seeing how each other's minds worked. If you didn't have a story to tell, a joke or brainteaser would do just as well in helping the night pass. Any friends who were visiting at the time our lights were off would often get caught up in our making the best of the situation, telling stories and talking about whatever was on our minds. We loved spending quality time with our mother and helping her get through the day with smiles on our faces. It was just an adventure for us. We would make plans, always seeing a better future. Just wait until tomorrow!

One of my fondest memories was a day just before the sun started to go down. My mother stopped playing a game with us and said, "I better start dinner before it gets too dark."

One of my friends looked at me and said, "I thought the lights were cut off."

We laughed and said, "Yeah, but the gas is still on, stupid!" Our friends had so much fun hanging with us and sharing their ideas, they wanted to know if our lights would still be off tomorrow and if they could come back. We were rarely embarrassed; we lived in the Kool-Aid house, where all the kids loved to hang out. Their parents liked knowing their kids were with us because they knew they were safe and fed. If we had food, they had food, no matter how little there was. Ramona was generous and kind. In nineteen sixty Black People were ready for change and Ramona was fearless.

She was the person everyone came to with their problems, big or small. She gave people tips on how to make the right decision. She really listened...she heard the things your mouth failed to speak. Everyone who met her came back for more. She expected the best from people, and that's what she got. If the subject was too difficult for our young friends to ask their parents, she would smooth the way by talking to their parents beforehand. She was the kind of person you could trust with your secrets. I never understood why my friends were afraid to talk to their parents. I could tell my mother anything. She may not have liked what I had to say, but I knew whatever the problem was, she would make it better. Ramona never turned any-one away; she didn't care if it was the last meal in the kitchen. Her motto was, when all the food is gone, God will provide. This taught us to be unselfish, and I can honestly say not a day went by without us eating something. Be it a friend who just happened to stop by and give her some money, or someone in the family who came around just in time to pay an overdue bill—by the grace of God, someone would show up. Like magic, they seemed to know when my mom would be running short. My Grandma Cootie, Aunt Linda and Aunt Loreen would show up many times with bags and bags of food. They would go shopping just for us. I found out later my big sister Pam would call them and tell them we needed help. My mother was a proud lady, and Pam knew she wouldn't say anything about our running short at the end of the month.

Whenever our grandmother would visit, Pam would always walk her to her car and tell her we needed food or the lights were getting cut off. Pam would ask Grandma Cootie not to tell our mother she said anything, because when our mother saw our grandma pulling up in the driveway, she would warn us all to keep our mouths shut. Our grandma would visit for hours and not notice anything was wrong. If Grandma Cootie asked our mother if she needed anything, she would say, "No, Cootie, I'm good."

On those rare occasions when she did accept help and the troops arrived….You should have seen the confusion on Grandma Cootie's and Aunt Linda's faces after they went shopping for us. As fast as we could, we got the food inside and put away. Then each of us would go back outside, sharing whatever they brought for us with our friends. They didn't understand that our friends were just as hungry as we were. It never occurred to any us to deny them.

My life is not a sad story. I grew up in a loving family with a strong support network. One of the great things about growing up in a Black neighborhood is you don't know prejudice. I was accepted everywhere I went. I was no different from the people on TV, even if they were all white. These were the days when everyone watching you was your mother and father. When every adult treated you like you belonged to them. If you were caught doing something wrong, you better hope that whatever you had done didn't get back to your parents.

If Mrs. Jackson had to say something to you, and your mother found out you brought shame on your family, which represented the whole Black race, that would mean double trouble because you would get it from Mrs. Jackson and your mother and father. Now you have a glimpse of my childhood.

These are some of the stories my mom shared that helped shape my life.

CHAPTER 2

Growing Up

47TH & BROADWAY

We grew up on 47th St. between Broadway and Main. The Annie Mae Apartment Building. I should say one of the many places we lived in Los Angeles. We moved around a lot. But this seems a good place to start. I was in the third grade and my big sister Pam was in the fourth. It was 1967, during the height of the Civil Rights movement when Black people couldn't get a good job or a fair shake and all colored people hated the police (a.k.a. the pigs).

Our landlord was a kindly white man who showed up twice a month to collect the rent and bribe the little kids with sweet pastries, pies and pocket change to help him keep the area around our apartment building clean. We always looked forward to seeing him. He was always good for a dime or a quarter. We had just moved into the Annie Mae Apartment Building. Living in a place with so many people was new to us. The Annie Mae Apartments had four apartments in the front and four apartments in the back. Each apartment had two bedrooms. Considering how many kids most families had, it amounted to a lot of people. My mother alone had six kids in a two-bedroom apartment, one for us kids and one for her. One lady in our building had thirteen kids in a two-bedroom apartment. This first story is about one of her kids named Big Debra.

CHAPTER 3

Big Debra and Ellen Pitts

Pam and I were afraid of Debra. She was around our age, but she was a bully the size of a grown woman. Our trouble started when I got into a fight with her little brother, Homer. I forget what the fight was about, but I was losing, and Pam jumped in to help me. Together we kicked Homer's butt. Homer was a good fighter, so after we beat him up, all the other kids on our block looked up to us. I guess Homer was a bully also. We had just moved to 47th Street from the San Fernando Valley. We'd gotten along well with all the kids in the Valley, so fights were rare.

After beating up Homer, we got the word Big Debra was looking for us. She was pissed because we double-teamed Homer. Every time Pam and I saw Debra, we hid from her or ran home. Our mother finally got sick of this on the day we ran off and left the groceries lying on the sidewalk. Thank God one of our friends gathered them up and carried them home for us. When our mother saw us coming, she locked us out of the house and said, "Today, you either fight Big Debra or fight me! Which is it going to be?"

We looked at each other and remembered Ellen Pitts. She was one of our mother's stories from her childhood.

31 BENNING PL.

Linda and Mona were getting ready for school. They were the same age as Pam and me, in the third and fourth grades, getting dressed and talking about how they were going to avoid Ellen Pitts on their way to school. They were tired of Ellen ambushing them and taking all the good stuff out of their lunch bag. Ellen was a big girl like Debra and bad news. She was always picking on the little kids, taking their milk money if she didn't like what they had in their lunchbox. Mama Jackson said she had a gland problem, and her mother kept all the food locked up to keep Ellen from eating too much. Mama Jackson always saw both sides of every story. She felt sorry for Ellen.

Maybe that's why none of the other parents ever talked to Ellen's mother about what she was doing to their kids; they felt sorry for her too. Mama Jackson had packed their lunches with all Linda's favorites today. Linda said, in her sweetest voice, "Mona, I'm not giving my lunch to Ellen Pitts today because I really like my lunch. If we run into Ellen, I just want you to know it's going to be a fight if she tries to take my lunch." That was code for "Mona, we are fighting today." Linda knew she couldn't beat up Ellen by herself. On their way to school, they looked around every bush, taking their time, dragging their feet, hoping Ellen would be gone by the time they left for school. But she was waiting for them and jumped out from behind a bush! "Let me see what you guys got for lunch."

"NO!" said Linda. "Ellen, I'm not giving you my lunch today because I really, really like my lunch." Ellen snatched Linda's lunch bag. And that's when the fight started! My mother said she and Linda climbed Ellen Pitts like she was a tree and bit her everywhere, in her head, on her arms, legs, and back. Ellen was screaming for help so loud everyone on the block came out to see what was going on. It took a lot to pull them off of Ellen. Linda and Mona clung to her for dear life. Ellen needed stitches all over her body, mostly her head. When Ellen got back from the doctor's, her mother called Mama Jackson to complain. She said Linda and Mona were dangerous and should be locked up. Her poor baby Ellen was scarred for life because of those animals. Mama Jackson told Ellen's mom not to call her again complaining about her granddaughters. She said, "I didn't call and complain when Ellen was bullying them every day and taking their lunches. As far as I'm concerned, Ellen got just what she deserved. She's been beating up the kids in the neighborhood and taking things from them for a long time. They should have beat her up a long time ago!" After my mom and Linda stood up to Ellen Pitts, no one else was afraid of her anymore. They knew her weakness and that their strength was in numbers. From then on, if Ellen tried to bully them, the kids would say, "If you try to beat us up, Ellen, we're going to do a Mona and Linda on you!"

4

Back to 47th Street

We would sit in the dark, candles lit, listening to our mother as she told us about Ellen Pitts and other stories of her childhood, how she coped with her problems growing up. We learned from her experiences how to cope with our problems, growing up in the ghettos of Los Angeles. She grew up in a middle-class environment in Dayton Ohio. We were less fortunate, yet in our childhood, the rules for survival were pretty much the same. Pam and I were ready. We had a plan. We were going to climb Big Debra like she was a tree and do to her what our mom and Linda did to Ellen Pitts.

We bravely walked up to Debra. Just when we were about to get her, our mother came running out of the house. She thought Debra was a grown woman. She said, "Aren't you too old to be picking on little kids? Let's see how big and bad you are fighting someone your own size." One of the kids in the crowd stopped our mother from hitting Debra just in time by telling her Debra was a kid, although you wouldn't know it by the way Debra was talking. She had no respect for adults, and my mother almost lost it. She grabbed Debra by the neck and asked her who her mother was. Then dragged her home to tell her mother how disrespectful she had been. She told her mother just how close her daughter came to getting beat down like a woman in the streets. Ester was Debra's mom. Ester thanked Mona and then pointed out all of her other twelve kids. She said, "Mona, feel free to beat the shit out any of them if they ever step out of line. I need all the help I can get."

Ester and our mother were best friends from then on. And so we're Pam and Debra. Debra thought Pam had a lot of guts to stand up to her like she did. Debra had a little brother named John who had MS (muscular dystrophy). He was confined to a wheelchair and drooled a lot. Whenever he saw Pam, his face would light up and his smile would stretch from ear to ear. Pam would walk over to him, wipe away the spit from around his mouth and bend down and kiss him. She would sit and talk to him like he was the only reason she came to visit. He loved her because he knew she loved him, wet kisses and all. It was the stories our mother told about people in her childhood who had disabilities and the lessons she learned from them that made us understand at an early age how important it was to look beyond the handicap to see the person inside.

THE DROOLING MAN

When Mona and Linda were young teenagers, there was a man their grandmother, Mama Jackson, knew who had a drooling problem. If he came by 31 Benning Place when Mama Jackson and Cootie were out, Mona and Linda wouldn't open the door for him. One day he came by just as they were closing the door to another guest, so he knew they were home. He walked up to the door and knocked, waited, knocked again. Still, they refused to answer, pretending they weren't home. He could see them inside; he knew they were hiding from him. They watched through the window as he hung his head and walked away. When Mama Jackson returned home, they told her he came by, but they left out how they hid from him and refused to answer the door.

Mama Jackson said she ran into him on her way back home and he looked hurt. This made them feel bad, so they told her the truth of what had happened. Mama was very disappointed in them. She said, "You two should be ashamed of yourselves! He is a good man... he was born like that... something that he can't help. Why do you think he chews paper all the time? How would you feel if you were like him and when people saw you coming down the street that's all

15

they saw? Not your eyes or your heart, just the drooling you were try-ing to control desperately by chewing paper?" My mom said she and Linda felt very small when Mama Jackson got through with them. They put themselves in his place and changed their ways after that. No more yucky faces when they looked at him. No more refusing to be in the same room when he was visiting. This was just one of the stories my mother used to teach us the value of treating people with respect. This story helped Pam to see inside John and treat him with a little kindness. She made him feel special, and her actions helped other kids in the apartment building see John like the little boy he was, not his handicap.

DELORIS

Deloris was a girl who got hit by a car and was in a coma for a year. She had scars on her face and a metal plate in her head, and she talked very slowly. After waking up from the coma, she had to learn how to walk and talk all over again. The kids at school ran from her all the time, treating her like a monster. Deloris hated the way she was treated, so she would chase after them. They liked to pretend they were afraid of her—everyone except my mother. Ramona Jane Cunningham didn't play like that. She knew that although Deloris was slow, she knew right from wrong. One of her sayings was if you were big enough to give a lick, you were big enough to take one. Mama Jackson described Mona as a mean child. Whenever her friends were visiting with small children, Mama Jackson would tell them, "Keep your teething child away from Mona because if that child bites her, she will bite him back."

One of Mama Jackson's friends had a toddler who had a habit of biting people. Mona tried to avoid the child, but the kid kept following her and biting her. She told the mother of the toddler that the baby kept biting her, and the lady said he's just teething. So the next time he bit her, she bit him back. The baby was screaming and holding his arm. My mother said, "I told you your baby was biting me and all you kept saying is he's teething, so I bit him back to show him how it feels." That was the last time that baby bit anyone.

I grew up biting little kids back who bit me. They were broken from that habit real fast in our family. It worked for our mother, and it worked for me...call it abuse if you want to. One day Deloris was chasing some kids on the school playground and ran into Mona, knocking her books out of her hands. She told Deloris to watch where she was going, but Deloris was upset she couldn't catch the person she was running after and took it out on Mona. Deloris hauled off and hit Mona, and of course, Mona hit her back. She hit Deloris so hard she was knocked to the ground. Just then a teacher showed up, seeing only Mona's part of the encounter, and chewed her out for hitting Deloris. The teacher said Mona was wrong for hitting Deloris because she had a metal plate in her head. The teacher said, "One day Deloris is going to snap, and when she does, Mona, you're going to be the first person she comes after."

Deloris picked herself up off the ground and said (in her slow voice), "That's not true. Mona is the only one who's not scared of me; she treats me like everybody else. Mona is my friend." Mona told Deloris to stop chasing kids and acting like she was crazy and maybe they would start treating her like everyone else too. My mother taught the teacher and Deloris a lesson that day. She said she and Deloris became good friends, and the other kids treated Deloris better when they realized she wasn't going to chase them and play crazy anymore. I learned from these stories to look people in the eyes. The eyes are the windows of the soul. Treat people the way you want them to treat you, not the way they are treating you.

I passed down these stories to my kids, hoping they would learn from them and become better people. I wasn't quite sure they got the message until one day their actions brought tears to my eyes. I watched them (Aaron, Brandon, and my nephew Kraig) talk to a little boy a friend was taking care of who had MS. He had no voice, and he couldn't walk; his eyes were his way of communicating. He would blink once for yes and twice for no. I watched them hold a one-way conversation, answering for him when the question involved more than a simple yes or no. They talked about how they would play in the swimming pool the next time he came to visit. He was free in the water. Floating on the surface of the water he was just like the other kids. I watched them look into that little boy's eyes and see that he was just like them inside. They saw not his deformity but themselves trapped inside with him, without a voice or movement. They treated him the way they would want to be treated if their roles were reversed. I saw the understanding pass between them as they smiled at each other. It was one of my proudest moments. I knew they were going to be good men...protectors of the weak, valiant, and strong.

CHAPTER 5

Maceo "Cat" House

When I was growing up, my mother's common-law husband, Cat (living together for eight years is considered common law), had a sister and a nephew who were mentally handicapped. They were the sweetest people in the world; all they wanted was to give you love. They didn't know the meaning of the word "retarded," but if you pissed them off, the first thing they would say is you called them retarded. The funniest thing was to watch them fighting and call each other retarded. It would go something like this: "You retarded." "No! You retarded." "You retarded!" "No! You retarded."

Someone in the family would usually stop the fight by telling them, "Shut up! You both are retarded!" My siblings and I never did this. "Retarded" is a bad word, and my mother would beat the snot out of us for treating them unkindly.

HARRY AND RICHARD'S MOM

Growing up, we were taught to serve those with greater needs. When someone died, it was our job was to bring food to feed the family of the deceased and work from the time we arrived until the time we left to go home. Our mission was to take care of the little things in an effort to ease the burden of grief. Pam and I would clean the common area of the house, bathrooms, kitchen, living-room and serve the family and friends. Encouraging them by showing them we cared and they were not alone in their grief. Ramona was the person everyone depended on in times of need, which means she was always volunteering Pam and I to help out also. And we were glad to be of service. She often told us stories of how Mama Jackson and her Mother Cootie (Susanna Cunningham) would assign them duties when helping sick people. Mama Jackson was an Eastern Star of the Masonic Order, which meant there were always duties to perform.

There was a lady who was bedridden with two boys Mona's and Linda's ages. It was the girls' job to clean the house, wash, and iron. Mama Jackson usually took care of the lady's personal needs and made sure the family had enough home-cooked meals for the week. The Eastern Stars took turns caring for their sickly sister until she was able to care for herself. Mona and Linda said they got tired of her sons watching them do all the work. The boys thought all they had to do was the heavy lifting and the dirty work. Mona and Linda started telling them what pigs they were and how they should be ashamed, living like pigs all week waiting for them to show up.

They said the boys thought cleaning and ironing was women's work. They replied, "This is not women's work; it's just work." They ended up teaching the boys how to clean and iron clothes. Mona said, "Harry and Richard never did learn all the things that needed to be done every week, but they got better." They also learned that with the four of them working together, the jobs took half the time. Together they developed a system, and as a result, they had more time to play.

By the time Harry and Richard's mom got well, her sons were well-trained and continued to help her around the house during her recovery. Richard and Harry also came in handy whenever Mona and Linda wanted to have a party. Cootie's only rule was the house had to be clean, before and after the party.

This attitude endeared Cootie to the boys in the neighborhood. She was not only one of the sexiest moms on the block, she was also the most fun to be around. It was same for us. Everyone loved to be around Mona.

CHAPTER 6

Church

We grew up with these two rules: 1) Saturday was cleaning day and nobody went outside until their work was done. We usually finished cleaning by noon. 2) Sunday was the LORD'S DAY. If you didn't go to church, you didn't go anywhere. Playing sick never worked because after church let out, you still couldn't go anywhere.

Pam and I loved going to church. We would always arrive early to Reverend Palmerton's house because Mrs. Palmerton always made homemade biscuits with Brer Rabbit syrup. Pam and I would eat at least half of the food before the Palmertons' children would wake up. The boys would always complain because there weren't enough leftovers for seconds after Pam and I finished eating. Mrs. Palmerton would just say, "I told you to get up before Pam and Kay got here." And smile at us for making her point. We beat them every time...and she never refused to give us more as we stuffed our faces. We were a lot younger than her children, and everyone spoiled us.

We loved to dance and knew all the latest moves; this made us everyone's entertainment. Whenever our mother had company, we would be called out of our room to dance for her guests. This was the only time we were allowed to be involved in grown folk's conversation, and we loved the attention. It's no wonder we would break out in the latest dance moves in church when the choir sang. Our mom would try to make us sit down, but the preacher would tell her to leave us alone; we were making a joyful noise unto the Lord. The Palmerton's started their church in the Garage in back of their home until the church was built. Baptist or Protestant I wish I could remember.

CHAPTER 7

Fights!

Mona and Linda were as close as two sisters could be. Maybe that's why they were always fighting. They were less than two years apart and looked as different as night and day. Pretty much like Pam and I. Mona had jet black curly hair, skin color so light it would make you do a double take—"Is she black or white?" Pam got my Mom's hair, only hers was silky and straight. I took after my father and got his snapback hair. Linda was tall and slim and had the typical soft unruly hair of most Black people. Mona was known for her big legs from an early age. Linda was known for her free spirit and sharp dressing befitting a model. It was usually clothes that led to their fights. They shared clothes, but Linda was slim, and Mona was curvaceous. Linda would ask Mona if she could wear her outfits first when they were new, or when they had just come out of the cleaners. Her reasoning was that Mona was shaped differently; the clothes would hang on Linda if Mona wore them first. Mom said she would let Linda have her way most of the time if she wasn't angry with her for something. That's when she would use her clothes to punish Linda. And that's when the fights would start. Because Linda would wear what she wanted to anyway.

Mona knew she could beat up Linda; she just never wanted to hurt her. Mom said she used to let Linda win.

I used to let Pam win our fights for the same reason; I also wanted the fights to end quickly because if our mother found out we were fighting, we would both end up getting a whipping. I would wear Pam's clothes without her permission because I knew she would say no. I would wear everything she had, including underwear, and I didn't care if I matched. I had no sense of style. Pam would always wait until I was with one of my friends and try to embarrass me by asking me if I had her underwear on. I would deny it, of course, and the fight would be on because she would ask me to let her see. I remember crying after one of our fights and her telling me to be quiet or Mom would hear me and we'd both get into trouble. I told her, "I don't care if you get a whipping, even if it means I get another one."

Mona finally got tired of letting Linda beat the stuff out of her. One day Linda came after her, and she didn't hold back. That's when the fights stopped for good. Linda and Mona would still argue, but no more blows were thrown. My mother warned Pam of the time when I, too, would get sick of her beating me up and take my revenge. I did get tired, but I never did beat her up. I would just sit on her until she calmed down. This is when she started calling me Baldy Bee to hurt my feelings. I think that insult was worse than the fights. Name-calling made me think I was ugly. And it didn't take long for all the other kids to pick up on this insecurity of mine and use it to hurt me too. I had a tiny Afro when it was not popular for little girls, a result of all my hair falling out when I was seven years old.

CHAPTER 8

Big Al

You ever hear of a seven-year-old girl having a nervous breakdown? Well, I was that little girl. Before we moved to 47th Street, we lived on Exposition Boulevard, in an apartment with two bedrooms. Albert Leonard Moore (aka Big Al) was Ramona's third love. He met our mother when we lived in the Projects of San Fernando Valley, she had three little girls when Al met her. She was divorced from Alto Lark, Pam's and my father and also husband #2, Cliff Williams, our younger sister Lettie's father. (Lettie is short for Lilette.) Big Al gave Mona the son she always wanted, Little Al. Little Linda came shortly after, named after Aunt Linda. Big Al was the first father I remembered. He was a good man.

My mother said she divorced Cliff because he was cheap and wanted to use all his money to take care of his family but never had anything left to help my mother's family. She said the final straw was when he wanted to treat Pam and me differently from the way he treated Lettie. Cliff wanted her to shop at the secondhand store for Pam and I, but for Lettie he brought everything brand-new. Mom said, "No man is going to treat her kids differently. We are a package deal. Love us all or get to stepping." She left our father Alto—Pam's and mine—because he wouldn't be faithful to her. She said, "I can be miserable all by myself, I don't need any help." Big Al was the third man my mother fell in love with, but after two failed marriages, she refused to marry again. She told Al they could live together, but marriage was out of the question. You could never tell by the way he treated us that he wasn't our father. He was the kind of man children were drawn to. He worked at the local park as the athletic director and was loved by all. Whenever Pam and I had a fight with the other kids, we would run to him thinking he would take our side. We would tell the kids that our daddy was going to kick them out of the park. We thought we had power because our father was running things. But he never took sides when we ran to him, and we never felt at a disadvantage. He was good at making peace, and after talking to him the argument would soon be forgotten.

My first taste of reality came after Pam and some of our friends watched me eat a green apple. We were outside of our apartment on the side of the building playing when Pam went upstairs to our apartment and asked Al if we could have something to eat. He asked her how many of us were outside and counted four green apples. This was to hold us until the next meal. Pam looked at all the apples and picked the best one for herself. We all grabbed one, and I noticed I was the only one eating.

They all waited until I finished my apple then Pam told me I ate the apple with the worm in it. I said, "I don't care. It was good, and I'm going to ask if I can have another one."

I opened the door to our apartment to see my mother rushing out of her bedroom tying her belt to her bathrobe. She took one look at me and said, "I'm going downstairs to make a phone call. Don't go in there!" I waited long enough for her to get to the bottom of the stairs of the neighbors' apartment, where she was making her phone call, before I knocked on her bedroom door. I wanted that second apple bad, and I knew my daddy would give it to me. I waited a moment for his voice to say come in; no sound. When my knock went unanswered, I knocked harder, and the door drifted open.

I went inside and walked around to Al's side of the bed. He was lying on his side with his back to me. I tapped him on his shoulder, but he didn't respond... I pushed him once, and he floated over onto his back. He looked asleep until his nose started to bleed. I watched in horror as his nose bled with so much force, his nose looked like it split in half, straight down the middle. The next thing I remembered was my mother pulling me out of the bedroom. I don't remember how I got outside the front door. I was standing in the stairway with everyone else. The firemen and police were in our apartment doorway trying to keep everyone from getting in the way. The stairway was full of people, adults and kids all wanting to know what was going on, wanting to help in some way. I broke through the crowd and the police barring the door and ran through the firemen just in time to see the paramedics bounce Big Al off the bed onto the floor to start CPR.

I returned to the living room where my mother was asking anyone who would look at her, "Is he dead?" No one would answer her. No one would look at her. No one wanted to break the bad news to her. No one wanted to tell a woman who was eight months pregnant that her man was dead.

She took one look at me as I walked out of her bedroom and asked again, "Kay, is he dead?"

I didn't know what dead was; I was only seven years old, but I knew the answer was yes, so I said, "Yes, Mama, he's dead." I was the bad news breaker. Her mournful wail was proof of it. We moved in with my Grandma Cootie for a little while after Big Al died. My mom just couldn't go back to the place where Al died while they were making love. I remember her crying every morning when she woke up without the smell of coffee in the air. A constant reminder that AL'S DEATH was no nightmare she was going to wake up from. He was really dead! Because if he were alive, she would have coffee waiting for her when she opened her eyes first thing in the morning. Ever since they moved in together, coffee was always waiting for her when she took her first waking breath.

It broke my heart to see her in such pain. We kids tried to stay outside, away from the sorrow in everyone's eyes, away from the hurt our mother never seemed to recover from. And no one seemed to be able to help her. I thought I would never see her smile again... Grandma Cootie finally told our mother, "If you don't stop grieving so hard, you're going to lose your baby." This made Mona pull herself together and move on to the next step in grieving.

Al's funeral was the second one I attended: Mama Jackson's, was the first (my great-grandmother). At Mama Jackson's funeral, we were sitting in the front row, I on one side of Big Al, Pam on the other. We were dozing off, and he kept saying to us, "Wake up. Don't you want to say goodbye to your great-grandma one last time?"

I saw her casket, but it never occurred to me she was inside. I don't think I stayed awake long enough to see her. Our baby cousin Moe had already died, but Pam and I didn't go to his funeral. Our mother thought it would be too much for us to understand. At Big Al's funeral, when I saw him lying in his casket, I remember wondering why he was sleeping in church. He would always wake us if we fell asleep during the service. And after the service was over everyone walked out and left Al sleeping in church. I didn't understand why we were leaving him, and I wanted to be with him. "I want to go with my daddy!" I said.

Someone in the crowd said, "He's not your daddy."

I don't remember who said it, but my reply was, "HE is my daddy! Why would you say that?"

CHAPTER 9

Mean People

People can be so mean when you need them to be nice. At the graveside as they lowered his casket in the ground, and I asked, "Why are they putting him in the hole?" no one answered me. This confused me even more. I was a seven-year-old child, but I felt it was somehow my fault everyone was so sad. I shouldn't have told the truth! I should have stayed out of the bedroom as she told me to. Soon afterward, every time my mother combed my sandy-blond hair, it would come out by the handful. We girls, Pam, Jewel and I, used to wear our hair with a part down the middle with two cornrows, one on each side. On Sunday our mother would dress us up for church, and we would get bangs and a ribbon with our cornrows. It finally got to the point my hair was so uneven my mother had to cut it all off. No more cornrows for me! My new nickname became Baldy-Bee, thanks to Jewel... one day when she got mad at me the name just stuck. I felt ugly. My hair was so short I looked like a boy, with my body all lanky and slim. My Aunt Loreen and my mother decided to make me a wig. My head was too small for a store-bought wig, so they had to make one for me. I was happy as a lark. I could wear it in a ponytail or down if I wanted. This lasted for a few months until the wig started to lose its hair. Then there I was again, back where I started, Bald-Dee Bee. I made up my mind then and there that I would never make fun of people who couldn't help themselves. I always tried to imagine myself in the other person's place. My mother said I have too much empathy. I couldn't turn off my feelings as a child and as a result would feel the pain of others. I felt that if I prayed at bedtime, no one would die, and it seemed it was the days I forgot to pray that someone would die.

I didn't feel good about myself again until Aunt Linda turned me on to Twiggy, a high-fashion model with shorter hair than mine. All of a sudden I was in style, with a body like a boy, tall and lanky. I was model material. I was like Auntie Linda now, only with short hair. Our family had to deal with a lot of death during this time. Mama Jackson, Moe (Loreen's firstborn son) and Big Al all died around the same time. The youngest went first, Moe at three months of age. My mother said the Angel of Death, which looked like a dark shadow, came to their house and was walking towards Mama Jackson's room and turned around and went into Moe's. Mama Jackson had pancreatic cancer and died at home like she wanted.... Moe had pneumonia.... Big Al had high blood pressure and died from an aneurysm in his late twenties. That's why all my hair fell out, too much sadness and pain, too many changes for a little girl. Now I know how you can be drowning in sorrow, barely hanging on yourself and unable to help anyone else...My mother, Mona, was handling too much pain for one person; she couldn't focus on anyone else.

CHAPTER 10

47th Street

Lights are out again, and I go get candles from the local store. MOM, TELL US ANOTHER STORY ABOUT WHEN YOU GREW UP.

Mom-Mona, "Everyone said I was mean when I was younger. I just didn't take any mess! I never started a fight, but I would always finish one. There was this little girl who used to pull on my clothes all the time. I asked her to stop many times before she tore them. I even told her I was going to whip her behind when she did. I knew it was just a matter of time. Every time she did it, I would warn her, but she just kept on pulling on my clothes, and one day she tore my skirt. I walked over to the tree, very calmly, and picked a switch. I whipped her with that switch until her blouse was bloody and stuck to her. They had to cut it off. After that, the adults labeled me crazy. They didn't understand your Grandma Cootie was the sole support of the family and nice clothes were acquired by sacrifice. That meant eating beans until the next payday. I loved beans, but Linda didn't love them as much as I did!

"Mama Jackson took care of us while Cootie worked, so if we got into trouble, it was Mama who smoothed things over. We had this nosey neighbor who was always telling on us and all the other kids in the neighborhood. One day we decided to get her back. We called every business we could find in the phone book that delivered. We placed orders for everything we could think of and had it delivered to her address. We ordered food and we even ordered animals. I

31

think we ordered a monkey! Linda was sick upstairs, so we kept going upstairs to get her input when we ran out of ideas.

We were peeking out the window every time she received a new delivery, laughing our heads off. She knew it was us and called to tell Mama Jackson. Mama didn't believe her and said, "You need to stop accusing my grandchildren of doing something they didn't do! Linda is sick upstairs, so I know she couldn't be involved. My grandchildren would never do anything like that!" If she had asked us, we would have told her we were guilty. We never lied to Mama. When she found out it was us, she made us go over and apologize, but the neighbor refused to accept it.

She said, "Janie Bell, you think your grandchildren are little angels and never do anything wrong! That's why they're out of control!" Mama knew what we were capable of…she just made the mistake of not asking us first before talking to the neighbor. She believed us before anyone else.

I said, "That's why you believed me! When I was babysitting for Lois (our neighbor) and her money went missing, you asked me if I took it and when I said, 'NO, Momma, I didn't take it,' you looked at her and said, 'Kay didn't take your money; you better look elsewhere!' When I realized what she was talking about I told her I put her money under the doilies on the table because her daughter kept playing with it. If she had asked me first, I would have told her where it was. Mom, you always put your money under the doilies, so I thought everyone else did too." Mona said, "She had the nerve to ask if you would babysit for her after that, and I told her never again!"

It was a time like no other living in the Annie Mae Apartments. Someone was always running from the police, and we had a blind spot where our bedroom windows were located. We would fool them every time. No one trusted the LAPD; it was a time of unrest. The police were on our street so often doing raids looking for the person who fit the description. The Black men and boys would scatter, running in all directions. Mona would let the first ones to knock on our door come inside to help them outrun the police. They would run in the front door and out our bedroom windows. Both bedrooms looked out on either side of the apartment. One window opened towards the back parking area; the other one looked out on the side of the building walk way to the back apartments. The police were in the front, knocking on doors they thought the young men had run into. Not the side or back. My mother knew her rights and would talk to the officers in such a fashion of logic when they knocked at the door, they would always apologize for bothering her and us.

She got tired of the constant raids and went down to the local police station to complain. They showed her a map with a red dot around our neighborhood. The captain said to her, "Look, lady, you live in the red zone. This is a high-crime area and you are too nice to be living there. If I were you, I would get my children out of there? The raids are not going to stop!"

We moved shortly after Lilette started calling the mailman the check man. It seemed no one was interested in the mail until the first and the fifteenth. On these days the poor mailman couldn't even get a clear path to the mailboxes to put the checks in.

Everyone wanted to grab theirs right out of his hand. Poor people with depleted food supplies and hungry kids? Us included.

This is where she met Cat. Maceo House was his legal name; he was fun. She met him through Ester (Debra's mother). It didn't take long for him to move in with us. David was a baby with cold black curly hair, a chocolate complexion, and tight eyes like all the rest of us. Cat claimed David as his own; he looked the most like Cat, and people were always assuming David was his child. David's biological father threatened our mother by telling her if she ever got pregnant by him he would take his child from her and raise him. David never knew who his dad was because she couldn't take that chance of losing him.

My mother needed a man living on 47th Street who was her opposite; she was from the Midwest, kind and overeducated. Cat was from Texas, used to carrying a gun, with a fourth-grade education, but a master's degree in common sense! Cat could read everyone and did not play! They were a good team, Mona and Cat, and he loved us. He had to leave his children behind in Texas, so he gave us all the love he wanted to give them. He came from a large family, and we inherited them when we got Cat. They used to have some crazy family fights! Brother against brother, uncle against nephew: it would be all-out war.

Cat warned my mother if one of his sisters tried her in a fight to go for blood because that's the only way they would respect her. He said they beat up all his other girlfriends. He, Cat had no problem hitting his woman if she stepped out of line. He grew up in that type of household. This was a time when women had to fight back or be ruled, and Mona was still mean and refused to back down from a fight! Cat and she used to fight about him not working. All six of us children would listen as the argument escalated. We'd know when he was going to hit her. We knew because her words cut deep and that's all she had as a weapon to hurt him. She had black eyes all the time. She knew women who were in the same predicament as she and reached out with understanding to them. Her friend Mary was one of them. She had three kids—two girls and one boy, Lorenzo. I was in junior high school when they came to live with us. Pam was in the eighth grade, and I was in the seventh. One day when a fight broke out about Mary living with us, Mom told him she paid the bills! That's when the fight started! Lorenzo asked us, "Why do you let him get away with hitting your mother? It's more of you than him! If I had help, no one would hit my mother ever again!"

CHAPTER 11

Spanyata Bottle

This made us think. And we started to plan for the next time. We gathered the empty Spanyata bottles. These were large glass Jennie like shaped bottle that cheap wine came in. We had the little kids fill them with dirt for us. The grownups thought it was cute the way they filled the wine bottles, making funnels and digging with home-made tools. It looked like play to them. They had no idea of our plans.

We hid the weapons in the bushes and waited for the next fight. They argued a few times, but no fight broke out, and we were glad. Then it happened; Cat had been drinking. There was no way we were skating this time. The fight started in the one bedroom, went through the closet and ended in the bathroom. We gathered our bottles. He pulled out his gun to threaten our mother, and we started beating him with everything we had! I think Pam was the most vicious. I grabbed the gun as it slid on the floor and ran and hid with it next to a house surrounded by bushes and trees. I waited until Pam and my mother called my name. Only then did I come out of hiding.

My mom called Cat's brother, Emanuel, to come and get him.

His sister came instead, but Cat refused to leave our house. She called Emanuel and said, "You should see what they did to him! Come and get him before they kill him!"

Emanuel said, "Didn't anyone care when he was kicking Mona's ass! I ain't doing shit!" The next day, Cat called all of us inside the bedroom where he was recovering from his beating and apologized.

He said, "My father and mother used to fight when I was little, and I know how you all feel. I'm sorry, and if you forgive me, I promise I will never hit your mother again!" He was crying through his one eye that was closed, and the tears were bloody. He had bruises and knots on both sides of his head, lip busted, and those were just the injuries I could see. He stayed in bed for at least a week. I felt so sorry for him, I forgave him on the spot. Pam wanted him to suffer!

He was lots of fun, like I said, and true to his word he never hit our mother again. They would still argue now and then, but no blows were ever thrown. If we had food left over after dinner, whoever woke up first got to eat it. If the dinner was one of Cat's favorites, he would set a trap to stop whoever beat him waking up. Linda and Al (little Linda and Little Al) would always be the first ones up. Little Al was hip to Cat, and he and Linda would get through the traps without a sound. Cat would string thread through pots and pans so when thread was pulled or walked into, the noise would wake everyone up. He would often forget about the traps and set them off himself. We would wake up laughing, hearing him cuss and try to detangle himself. He was fun! At night when we were told to go to sleep, Cat would wait for the perfect time to scratch on our window outside. As soon as we noticed and got quiet to listen, he would yell out a roar and scare us! We knew it was him. He was just letting us know he knew we were not asleep.

—⚊ϡ⚊—

624 W. 55TH STREET

As we grew older and started to date, Cat would sit in the living room where Pam and I had our dates and pretend he was passed out drunk. To add to the illusion, he would be holding a Schlitz Malt Liquor bottle. The next day he would tell Pam and me what was said and what he didn't like about our friends. We would be in shock, wondering how we'd acted and what we said. When a boy got too close to us, if Cat was awake, he would sigh or turn over on the couch. Just enough movement to make the boys back off.

After we got hip to Cat, our boyfriends would try to sneak a kiss, and we would say no and tell them in a whisper, "He's not asleep!" Then Cat would just get up and go to another room. Making sure the boys knew what time to leave by tapping his watch as he got up, smiling at us because we didn't fall for his playing possum. He was the kind of father who demanded respect for his daughters.

There was this boy from my high school, Manual Arts! Purple and Gray, baby! Our school colors. Anyway, he was fine (aka handsome). The definition of "fine" at the time was light-skinned with a big Afro. I had been trying to get his attention for what seemed like forever. He was finally outside my house driving his cool car and honking his horn for me to run out. I was halfway to the door when Cat said in a don't-ask-me-why voice, "Where do you think you're going?"

"Outside, Daddy, my friend is here."

"DON'T NO HOES LIVE HERE! Sit your ass down."

I sat on the couch and listened until the horn stopped honking and said, "Daddy, he's going to leave."

Cat just shook his head. "No, he won't."

My date for the evening came to door, saw me sitting down on the couch and said, "Didn't you hear me honking?"

Before I could open my mouth, my father said, "Do you think hoes live here?"

My date was at a loss for words at first, but quickly recovered and said, "No, sir!"

"You must think hoes live here because I know you're not honking your horn for my daughter!"

"We're running late, sir, that's why I honked. It will never happen again."

"I'm trusting you to take care of her. She is a lady, and I expect you to treat her like one. Do you understand me?"

"Yes, sir, I understand." He introduced himself, told Cat what kind of goals he had for the future and what time he would have me back home. Short and sweet.... He was in awe of my father. My date was the perfect gentleman that night, opening doors for me and lighting my cigarettes and joints. He made me feel like I was precious. I never will forget that feeling. It showed me what to look for in a man.

Another one of my dates came to pick me up as Cat was cleaning his gun! My date thought it was cool. He talked about the parts of the gun and what type of bullets it took until Cat asked the young man, "What does the writing say on the side of the bullet?" The boy said .45 or something like that, and Cat said, "No, this bullet has your name on it if you hurt my daughter!" That warning went for my feelings as well as my physical form.

Maceo "Cat" House was the only man Ramona quit and took back. She was tired of us running short every month and him sitting at home, not working. She told him she needed help and if he wouldn't get a job, she was through! No one would help her with Cat living with us. He had a time limit to get out that came and went, and he was still living with us. She told him they were now roommates, and he was to be introduced as the babysitter if asked. All because he refused to get out! She said, "Cat, I'm going to start dating other men. I need to find someone who can help me as well as love me. So I'm telling you, when my date shows up, you better not trip out on him." Cat huffed and puffed, but she stood her ground… Cat couldn't take the competition. Seeing her drive off with another man was too much for him.

He moved out and found a job working at a local gas station. He got his own apartment, and Mom and Cat dated for a few months before she let him come back home to 624 W. 55th Street. A home my mother bought with the help of her kind Jewish employer, Meryl.

She started off as an assistant to the optometrist in a local medical office. It didn't take long for her to excel in her field and become the administrative assistant for the whole medical building. Everyone loved her because she could communicate with people of all types. She was intimidated by no one!

—◆—

39TH STREET AND WESTERN TEXACO GAS STATION

We worked from time to time for our father when Cat was short-handed. Pam and I were teenagers growing in beauty each year and aware of our power over the opposite sex. We worked in the gas station, but we refused to pump gas for the male population. We took care of the ladies. I guess we were forward-thinking because we never thought self-serve gas stations would take off like they did. We were one of the first, without even thinking about it. Guys would show up just for a quarter of gas: that's 25 cents. Yeah! Gas was cheap back then. Pam and I always had dates for the weekend, and Cat knew this. One day we worked for eight hours, and his next shift was MIA. Cat called the station to tell us we had to stay until he found our replacements. We told him he had until the end of our shift; or we were taking inventory and closing the Texaco gas station on 39th Street and Western down! We never got robbed because we set straight all the ones who thought we were too dumb to know they were casing our operation. We told them in our innocent way when and why we dropped the money in the underground safe. "Aren't you ladies afraid of people trying to rob you?"

"They can have the funky $20. This isn't our gas station!"

"All you have is $20 in that drawer?"

"YES. Every time we make about that much money, we drop it in the safe. We don't have the key to the safe or we would give them the money in there too!" We would even show them the safe sometimes if they kept coming back with more questions.

CHAPTER *12*

Little Al

Little Al would make money letting people who ate at the popular breakfast spot just across the street park in the gas station. They even paid him to run and tell them if someone tried to break into their rides. He had a good little business and was always working on the weekends. He had regular customers he would save a spot for. Then the lot started to get too full, and it became a problem. All those cars, and we still had a gas station to run. Al's business was so good people were always trying to squeeze in one more car. We had to put our foot down! Our little brother, Little Al started a small business for the community, providing parking spaces.

Our home at 624 W. 55th Street was a small, cute two-bedroom house with one bathroom. It was on a large lot, and the house was located in the rear with a deep front yard. The front yard was so big we could have built another house on the front part of it. Mom had plans to expand by extending the front of the house towards the front of the street, adding all the extra bedrooms we needed. But we lost it in foreclosure. This was the longest time to date we had ever lived anywhere…. And we owned it…. No landlord could say we were too many living in a two-bedroom ever again. We went down swinging! Mom loaned our house payment to Aunt Linda so she could save her home. She didn't pay Mom back in time to save our own. We took all the work we could get at the gas station (Mona, Cat, Lilette, Pam, and me), trying to raise enough money to catch up on our mortgage before it was too late! Not Only because of Linda; but also the owner

40

of the gas station, who held up our paychecks because Cat's books were short. Cat had been floating the losses from one day to next as he was trained. The accountant who balanced the books instructed Cat on how to cover the losses each day. But the owner still wanted to take his losses out of our pay, regardless of what his accountant trained Cat to do. Mom met with the owner, explained why he was wrong by going over the records she kept. She had warned Cat what could happen when she realized what the accountant wanted Cat to do. She saw the problem well in advance and protected Cat from the backlash. She started keeping her own copy of the daily losses. At the meeting, she told the owner he was in for a large lawsuit if he didn't pay us. She said, "Regardless of what you have going on with Cat, my children and I worked and will have to be paid. When I sue, I will own one of these gas stations."

By the time everything was straightened out, we were too late to save our home. Pam and I were sixteen and seventeen when we lived on 55th Street, and she and Cat were always arguing. Mom refused to get in the middle of their fights. Pam had a child, Shonnie, and she was helping run the household while Mom was at work. This was during a time when Cat wasn't working, and Pam felt she had a say because she was the one helping Mom pay all the bills. I was moving out because I had fallen in love with Calvin, who was twenty-one years old and working for UPS. He roomed with his brother Earl in a two-bedroom apartment. I was studying to be a Jehovah's Witness, and marriage was in my near future. I was seventeen.

CHAPTER 13

Calvin

All I can say is don't rush into marriage! We were too different and too young! Due to my being underage, seventeen, I had to get the permission of both my parents. I was required to go to a marriage counselor as well as get permission from a judge to be approved for a marriage license. If I had been pregnant it would have been easy to get married, no questions asked!

I was new to the Truth and wanted to do things right. GOD'S way, marriage before sex. I had had three serious boyfriends before I met Calvin. I thought I was in love each time. Michael Hill was my first, then Paul and Gerald. Calvin was a virgin when we met, and throughout the seven-year marriage, he was resentful that he was not my first. I tried to be a good wife. I changed myself to fit his idea of the perfect homemaker. I cooked, cleaned, taught Aaron and Brandon right from wrong and waited for Calvin to come home. He worked the night shift as an LSM operator for the US Postal Service. It was a good job until he was fired from UPS at the beginning of our union. We struggled for a while. There was a clash between white and black in the workforce, and Calvin refused to bow down. His supervisor changed his mind about firing Calvin after he found out he had a young wife and a child on the way. Nevertheless, Calvin refused to give in to keep his pride.

We got married at the local courthouse because we couldn't wait any longer to be together. We were planning a big wedding and had decided to pretend we were not married and have two ceremonies.

We wanted everyone to be happy. For some reason, Calvin's mother, Marian, was holding our wedding rings. When we went to get them, she knew we were eloping and started crying. She was not my biggest fan; I knew she didn't think I was good enough for her son. I was the asset in this relationship... I was the one he needed... I loved him and tried to fill that void in him of not having a family growing up. My family was close, and we craved each other's company. Calvin didn't have this closeness growing up. He and his brother were raised by their father's side of the family. Calvin and Earl started out living with their grandparents because their mother was very young when she had them. After she and Earl Lasley Sr. split up, she left her sons with their father to go find work. While she was gone, Calvin and Earl Jr. were shipped around to their aunts and uncles. They felt unwanted. They were constantly reminded by their cousins they didn't belong because they didn't live with their father or mother. When Marian did return for them, they became latchkey kids, frequently left alone while their mother took care of other women's children. Calvin said on holidays his mother's idea of dinner was a hot link. It was all she had to feed them. After she married an Army man named Clark, things were better financially, but Clark was a strict man and wanted to shop at second hand stores for Calvin's and Earl Jr.'s clothes. This continued as they grew into young men and made them feel unwanted all over again.

They moved out as soon as they were old enough. It was those two against the world. They stuck together and made a living for themselves. Both were devout Jehovah's Witnesses. Calvin and I lived with my mother for a few months after Calvin lost his job with UPS. My mother loaned us the money we needed to move into a little bungalow duplex on 76th Street between Figueroa and Hoover. It was a big step down from the Lake Shore Tennis Club Apartments we started our marriage in. Our first place was a one-bedroom, one-bath, condo-style apartment, with a man-made lake running through it and tennis courts. We furnished our apartment with everything brand new. We bought furniture from the R&B Furniture Store. It was beautiful. Powder-blue couches and a dinette set to match, with chrome detail and glass tables, very modern and chic. A king-size bed with wood detail and end tables and a dresser to match.

706 1/4 WEST 76 STREET

On 76th Street we were no longer in upper-middle-class surroundings. We lived among the poorest and most desperate people imaginable—prostitutes, pimps, drug dealers and drunks. And to top it all off, the place was mouse-infested! Calvin set traps every night before leaving for work, and every night they would wake me, snapping, one after another. My neighbor would always come and empty the traps and re-set them for me. I couldn't sleep with dead things in the house. I would pay my neighbor back by fixing him a plate of food the next time I cooked a great meal. Everyone on the block looked out for me at night when Calvin worked. They treated me like I was special....

I was kind to everyone, and I spoke to everyone. They soon noticed that Calvin never spoke to anyone! How hard is it to say hello? One day an old man asked me, "Why doesn't your husband ever speak to us?" "You always speak." I asked him if that hurt his feelings that Calvin never said hello. He said, "Yes."

I told him, "The next time you see Calvin, he will speak to you." When I told Calvin how everyone looked out for me when he was at work and how he was hurting people's feeling by walking past them without speaking, he promised me he would speak from then on. After that, I was greeted with big smiles every time I saw the old guy as I asked, "Did my husband speak to you today?"

His answer was, "yes!"

Before Calvin found a job with the Postal Service, I was pregnant with Aaron, and we were living on Calvin's unemployment check, which was $95 every two weeks. It was just enough to pay our rent, lights or gas and buy food, never both utilities at the same time. We stayed with my mother in between checks.

When Calvin found out the Postal Service was hiring, he walked several miles every day to and from the training facility. This was just for the hope of becoming an LSM operator for the Post Office Processing Center. We couldn't afford the bus fare. He wore holes in his shoes walking. When he was in high school, he was a long-distance runner, so walking was easy for him. He walked from 76th street and Figueroa to Marina Del Rey. His day was just starting when he came home tired. He still had to study for the test on the following day. He was determined to make a better life for us. After he started working full time, he put one check a month in the bank, and we lived off the other. He got paid every two weeks, $800. We saved ten thousand dollars in one year to put towards buying our first house.

Both our sons, Aaron and Brandon, were born on 76th street. But before Brandon was born, Calvin started cheating on me. Working at the Postal Processing Center, Calvin started seeing a woman who worked with him. When I found out, I packed my things, took my baby (Aaron) and moved in with my mother. He ruined the relationship with his jealousy over my past! He always thought I was more experienced than him, and he needed to get even. The last straw was when he dated one of my little sister's friends. He met her at a club one night. The Hobart Club was on his way home, and he found her there. He didn't even know the girl he met was friends with Linda.

His little girlfriend had even been to our house selling clothes. Calvin never noticed her! Or did he? Our first house was on 55th street and Denker. My mother lived with us shortly after we bought our house. And Little Al, Linda, and David came with her. It was clear to me Calvin didn't want them there! He knew they would notice things I didn't. He was smoking cocaine and cheating on me. And I didn't have a clue. I was working as a nurse's aide/orderly at Kaiser Sunset and making my own money with good benefits. Brandon was three years old and Aaron was eight when I left their father for good! It was over when I realized I didn't love Calvin anymore. He killed my love with his mental abuse and infidelity. I no longer recognized myself when I left him. I had changed to be what I thought my husband wanted, a submissive wife. When he met me, I was a strong woman who spoke her mind and was the life of the party. I changed into a person who was a doormat, to be walked upon…I changed to make him happy, and he was sure I would stay. He said, "Who's going to want you with two kids?"

I said, "After being married to you, the last thing on my mind is a man! My mother took care of six kids by herself. I'm pretty sure I can take care of two." I was working full time and no longer a Jehovah's Witness. I was disfellowshipped after I started dating while I was still married to Calvin. It was an eye-opener for me to see how the elders felt about adultery. When they found out Calvin was cheating on me, they asked him, "Calvin, has Karen ever been unfaithful to you? I know you work the night shift, has it ever occurred to you she's been unfaithful?"

"No, not ever!" was Calvin's quick reply. "She would never do that!" He was so sure of his place in my life. It never occurred to him that my love for him had evaporated slowly over time because of my dealings with him and his lack of empathy for what he was putting me through. He was never content with just having me in his bed. He was always thinking of how he could even the score. I wanted to divorce him!

The elders asked me to give it another try. "After all…men do this type of thing. It's just a phase men go through." They totally understood his reason for cheating on me. I felt like they took his side. And even more, it felt like this was a rite of passage for a man to grow into manhood! We were living like roommates, him in the kids' room and me in ours. He thought I would give in, but I was determined to be happy again. I started dating a guy at work, and one thing led to another. I broke the rules and was disfellowshipped from the Organization of Jehovah's Witnesses. What this means is that everyone who is a Jehovah's Witness will shun you. No one will talk to you until you get reinstated, with the exception of family. I knew the rules and accepted my punishment. I was also disappointed in the Brothers, our Elders as well. I wanted to punish them with my absence. But I missed the friends instead…

ALL I EVER WANTED TO BE WAS A HOUSEWIFE AND
MOTHER!

Now I had to work! No turning back.... All the jobs I worked
when I was married, I quit for one reason or another. The main reason was Aaron needed me home. I knew Calvin was glad. He never
wanted me to work in the first place.

I was content living my new life, dating and partying with my
sister, Pam, and best friend, Marsha. Pam and I were roommates,
taking care of our children together and barely making ends meet,
but we were happy. There was little left to spend on ourselves, after
paying all the bills and buying food, but we never went without
lights or gas. Our mother was laid off at this time, and she was our
paid babysitter. Her rent was $200 a month, and Lilette, Pam and I
paid her more than that to keep our kids, although she would have
kept them for free. This was our way of helping her as she helped us.
We had no worries. Mom potty-trained all of her grandchildren she
babysat. When Aunt Linda sold the home we were renting from her,
Pam and I went our separate ways (not far). I found an apartment
on Cadillac (8933 apt #1) in Los Angeles, and Pam moved upstairs
from us, in apt three. My mother became my new roommate. Aaron
and Shonnie were in school, and Kraig (Pam's son) and Brandon in
pre-school, just down the block from Mom's new job. She took them
with her every morning on her way to work and picked them up
every evening after work. I was glad I had a job at Kaiser. I found my
lifelong friend, Marsha, working there.

Marsha. Marsha.

CHAPTER 14

Marsha

Marsha and I became close during her daughter Megan's stay in the hospital. Megan had leukemia and was admitted often for chemotherapy treatment. Marsha lived in Megan's room at Kaiser while Megan was hospitalized. Megan gave me another sister in Marsha and a baby girl in herself. I can't say enough about Marsha and her strength. She looked Death straight in the eye and did what she had to do. It's not easy to stop fighting when the day comes, even if you were told all along that it was coming. I never believed Megan was going to die either! This little girl would never pout on her bad days…. She'd lift you up with a smile that started in her eyes, then slowly spread to a wide almost-laugh! She was beautiful, and I fell in love with her long before I met Marsha She would throw up from the chemo, then keep on playing when she had the energy. The day Marsha let her go, I had just returned from a vacation in Hawaii with Ron (my new man friend who was thirteen years my elder). It was my first day back, and I saw all of Marsha's family spilling out of the room we reserve for farewells. I asked what room Megan was in and went to be by Marsha's side. Megan was in a coma on life support, yet she squeezed my hand as I talked to her. Marsha asked me, "Karen, what should I do? They want me to take her off life support." I said, "Marsha, I can't tell you what to do. How long has she been like this?" I don't remember her answer… I do remember her consoling me—instead of me consoling her—when I asked, "Why did she have to die today?"

Her response, "She waited for you, Karen." As we waited for Megan's heart to stop beating, Marsha held her in her arms like she was already gone. I kneeled down and started talking to Megan.

"Hi, Meg-a-leg. When you get to heaven, put in a good word for me." I don't remember all I said to my and Marsha's baby…but as I talked to Megan, Marsha pulled her closer and closer to her heart for the release Megan was waiting for and found peace. All I could do was cry all day at work. Hiding in empty rooms and bathrooms so Marsha wouldn't see, but Marsha's mom Madeline did. Everyone knew I loved her. She and Gashacoo were my favorites. Gashacoo was four years old when I kissed his feet. He was sad to be in the hospital once again and his depression was visible. I walked into his room to see him and his mom playing with Play-Doh… I told him I don't let my kids play with Play-Doh because it gets inside the cracks of my hardwood floors.

Then I said, "Can I kiss your feet?"

He said sadly, "Yes."

I grabbed his feet and gently pulled them to my face and kissed both his little feet several times, then I hugged his feet to my chest and said, "Do you know how special you are? I only kiss babies' feet. You are the only big person's feet I have ever kissed!" He smiled, and so did his mother… Gashacoo was half African (his father) and half white. They were a sweet family. When Gashacoo died, his father said, with wonder in his eyes, "Gashacoo went back to Africa.…"

Kaiser laid me off! What was I to do now? I tried private nursing, clerical work and was a part-time mail carrier. Then Marsha told me the fire department was hiring. They needed more minorities and women…

CHAPTER 15

The Los Angeles Fire Department

Cool, I was both! I ran to apply. In preparation for the job of Firefighter, the Department provided a voluntary workout with weights at night. I went after working all day as a postal worker. The training program was open to all recruits, but women were the target the program was designed for. To qualify as a firefighter, women need to build upper body strength, something most men have naturally. It was cool seeing my body respond to the weights and endurance training. The hardest thing to build was grip strength. You needed a good grip to pull the halyard. This is a rope attached to sixty-five-pound weights that had to be pulled up three times to a height of about twenty feet, then lowered in a controlled manner, hand over hand. No sliding through the grip! All this was done in preparation for the physical agility test, which is a series of exercises to simulate a day in the life of a firefighter and includes a step test, a hose drag, a hydrant connection, and an exercise that requires squat repetitive motions. Out of all these exercises, the halyard is the one that eliminates the most people.

Men were required to take a written test, but not women. The women in the Pre-Trainee Program were given a mock PAT (physical agility test) every month. Westlake Fire Training was the place firefighters were made. I hoped to get into the next pre-trainee class, a position paying about $900 per month. In 1985, that was good money.

PRE-TRAINING (WESTLAKE)

I was rooming with my mother. She worked as an office administrator, and I was in need of a babysitter for the boys. Being a firefighter is a twenty-four-hour job. Defeat was not an option. I had to make it for my sons. I ran every day and afterward worked out with my home-made weights. All to help me build muscle and endurance. My boyfriend at the time, Ron, was helping me workout and at the same time telling me I was wasting my time. I shut him up by asking if he was going to pay my bills.

At Westlake, I was told by Captain W. that they wouldn't pick me for the Pre-Trainee Program. After all my hard work! I said to him, "It's okay; I'll just take the written test like the men do and get in that way!" I could still work out at Westlake; it was open to the public. I said, "Now that I know I can be a firefighter, I am going to be one!"

He thought I was cocky and too outspoken. Not a good fit in a paramilitary organization. I put in an interest card on the spot and went back to working out with the weights. One of the girls I was working out with told me as soon as I turned my back, Captain W. tore up my interest card and threw it into the trash. I went back to the table where he was sitting and filled out another one, handed it to him and told him not to throw this one away! I was very girly looking, and they were looking for women who looked and acted more like men. I didn't fit their idea of a capable firefighter. I was six feet tall, 165 pounds, with long fingernails when Capt. W. saw me for the first time. He said, "You can't raise the halyard with those long fingernails! I asked him for scissors and clipped them right then and there. He didn't want to give me the scissors at first, saying his wife was going to kill him when she found out what he made me do.

THE WRITTEN

I took the written test at Hollywood High School. The line wrapped around the block. I was the only girl in line. The firemen giving the test kept trying to give me clues on how to answer the questions that I didn't know. Like, "Always pick C for the answer you don't know…" I don't know if it helped or not, but I passed the written and was ready to take the real PAT.

—m—

THE PAT

Again, on test day for the PAT, I was the only woman testing. First the step test, ten minutes of walking in a consistent manner, three steps back and forth, with sixty-five pounds on my back to simulate the equipment firefighters have to carry in high-rise buildings. I passed this part with an easy rhythm in my head.

Next…The halyard. I pulled it up once, smooth all the way. The second time was a little harder than the first, but I still had control, up and down. Now I had one more to go… the third time. I had to concentrate with every pull on the rope, hoping to make it all the way to the top and ring the bell that said I'd done it… but with one more pull to go and ring the bell and my goal, I knew if I let the rope go to reach hand over hand to pull it one more time, it would slip. I had lost my grip! Time ran out as I held on for dear life, hearing a guy behind me say, "Karen if you just bend your legs, it will ring the bell." If I had, he thought I would have passed.

It seemed everyone who worked for the fire department was waiting and watching to see how well I would do, Captain W. included. When I failed the PAT, he gave me the news. "We are not going to pick you. So give up. You can be anything, why do you want to be a firefighter?"

I said, "Because now I know I can be a firefighter! I'm going to be one. I can try again in a year. I'll be stronger, and I will make it next time."

I went after work every day I could to work out at Westlake. I was doing everything I could to be ready the next time. I was talking to one of the women who was my spotter and she was saying to me, "I don't like Captain W."

I asked, "Why?"

She said, "He is always watching us, and I don't like it!"

I said, "I don't like him either, but it's because I know he doesn't like me."

It was as if he read my lips because he walked over to me and said, "Karen, you don't have to come here anymore. We decided to put you in the pre-trainee program." I was thrown for a loop. He was giving me my chance to become a female firefighter. I was going to be able to provide for my children in the manner to which they had become accustomed. I was elated!

CHAPTER 16

Pre-Trainee Program

We started out with five women. Only two made it all the way to graduation. I was the only woman with the responsibility of kids to feed. Each day started with us washing away all the filth from the previous night's homeless people who used the steps as a public restroom. We used bleach and a water hose to wash it all down. It was also our job to wash all the cars of the inspectors who were working that day, usually about six or seven cars including that of Chief Baker, who was the head of the training academy. We were also assigned the daily housework…bathrooms, offices, vacuuming and emptying trash. After all our chores were done, we had strength-training and endurance training to improve cardio; this also included lifting weights.

A peer-group instructor was assigned to us. He was responsible for teaching us about tools and equipment as well as the rules and regulations of the Fire Department. It was a ten-hour day, Monday, Tuesday, Thursday and Friday. All in preparation for the drill tower. I was in a position that would change my life. I knew prejudice from growing up in the 1960s, but I thought that was all behind me. I thought I would be accepted in this field that needed minorities and women to represent the City of Los Angeles. Boy, was I wrong! (The consent decree was badly needed.) My peer-group instructor was not happy about the new consent decree. Out of the five women, I was the only Black one. He took his anger out on me by singling me out at every turn. If he wasn't downgrading me, he was ignoring me. In the classroom, he refused to call on me when I raised my hand. It got so obvious that the other women would raise their hands and when he called on them, they would say, "Karen has a question."

He would ignore that person and go to the next one who raised their hand, and that person would also say, "Karen has a question." I was upset but what could I do? One day when it was time for us to wash the inspectors' cars, I started before the other women, and when they filed out, one by one, after doing their housework, he detained them and told them not to help me wash cars today. He pretended he wanted them to do something else. They knew he was punishing me and were not happy about it! But what could they do? He was in charge. He told me I was going to wash cars today by myself.

I was pissed for a minute until I thought about how much they were paying me. I decided I was going to not just wash the cars but also detail them. I cleaned them so well every inspector that came out to get into his car commented on how much work I did and how good it looked. I had ten hours to wash cars, so I took my time and did a good job on all of them.

One day I was stretching my back by bending over while holding on to the weight machine. My peer-group instructor put his foot under one of my butt cheeks and tried to shake it! As if he couldn't believe my ass was as firm as it appeared. There was only one other person in the weight room with us when this happened to me. He was also a peer-group instructor. I was in disbelief when he touched me with his foot. I said, "Don't you ever touch me like that again!" He tried to laugh it off, but I told him, "Look at my face. I'm not smiling! Don't you ever touch me like that again! I mean it!" I also told the other peer-group instructor to make a note of this incident because it might come up again.

He said, "Duly noted, Karen." After that encounter, I couldn't hide my disdain. Before this incident, I would try to talk to him in a way that would make him see me as a person like any other. Now, everyone noticed the tension when I talked to him. And I would only talk to him if he asked me a direct question. No more raising my hand to be ignored! I was through with trying to make him like me. It all came to a head the day I was putting my name on my workout clothes. He approached me and asked me what I was doing. I said, "Stenciling my name on my uniform."

He asked me, "Why are you doing it now? Why didn't you do it when the other girls did theirs?"

I told him, "Because I was busy doing something for Chief Baker when the other girls did their stencils."

He asked again, "Why now?" I ignored him… He said, "Are you going to answer me?"

I said, "I would rather not." He got angry and told me to follow him into the captain's office. When we got to the captain's office, he told the captain I was being insubordinate, which is grounds for termination! The captain asked me what happened. I told him that I would not talk to him until my peer-group instructor left the room. He asked the instructor to go out and let us have a private talk. Under protest, the instructor left.

My captain said, "Karen, what's going on between you two? Everyone can see you have a problem with M." I told him (as my tears started to flow), "I've tried to get along with him, but he crossed the line when he put his foot on my ass! He has been mean to me the whole time, but I've been taught prejudice was due to ignorance. And when you know better, you do better. I've been trying to educate him about Black people, but when he put his foot on me that showed me how he feels. I can't hide how that made me feel. Spitting on and kicking a Black person is the worst insult you can inflict! Another peer-group instructor was present when it happened. If you don't believe me, you can ask him what happened…"

My tears were flowing freely now, and the poor captain started to tear up too, all the while asking me to stop crying. Captain Martinez told me, "You know you could have his job for that!"

I said, "I don't want his job. He has a wife and kids; what would they do if he lost his job? I just want him to understand I have children depending on me too!"

Later that day I was sitting on a bench eating my lunch alone. The asshole—peer-grouper M.—came up to me and said, "Karen, can I talk to you? Captain Martinez told me what you said when they offered you my job! I'm so sorry for the way I treated you. I was wrong. I was raised different, and I didn't think about what I was doing to you. Please accept my apology."

I did, and we never had another problem after that! He became one of my staunchest supporters in the fire service. But there were other opposers along the way! He was just the first of many!

WESTLAKE TRAINING

I passed the PAT in the pre-training program that they were preparing us for. And when we took the mock PATs, I never failed one when we practiced. We were next enrolled in the pre-drill tower at Westlake. This is where we were taught basics of ladder evolutions, knots and basic firefighting skills. For the first time in our training, we were training with the men who had passed the written test. After Westlake training, we started the drill tower. There are two drill towers. Drill Tower 40 is in San Pedro, and Drill Tower 89 is in the Valley of Los Angeles.

CHAPTER 17

Drill Tower

DRILL TOWER 89

This is where we were tested on ladders and learned the fire code. We also came back here after going to Drill Tower 40 to become emergency medical technicians. I did well on the written test because of my love of reading. One of the girls was told, "Karen is strong, but she will never pass the written exams." She replied, "You're wrong, because every spare moment, Karen was reading."

—◦◦◦—

LADDERS (STRAIGHT AND EXTENSION)

This was the first phase of the drill tower experience, and it was hard! I was never able to rest on ladder evolutions. There was one ladder, a twenty-foot wooden extension ladder, that was a little bit heavier than the others. We called it Bertha! The guys would give each other a break now and then by skipping Bertha and going to one of the lighter ladders lying on the ground next to it, but I never could! Everyone on the yard would watch my every move. I felt like a fish in a fishbowl. All of us were tired after going up and over, and I really hated it because I was always the last one to fall in line! YES. I hated it! Every morning after working out and running, we had to climb—or I should say run—up a ladder that was bolted to the outside of a six-story building. Going straight to the roof! Upon reaching the rooftop, we would shout, "Hand, foot, foot, hand!" This was the proper way to transfer from the ladder to the roof. It was a safety rule to prevent us from falling. We were always running, never walking, when we were on the yard. When coming out of the building, we lined up in formation. The first one down got to rest in line waiting for the rest of us to get down the stairs from the inside of the building we had just run straight up. When we all came down, we were told to go up and over again! Twice a day minimum…I never got a chance to rest because I was always the last one. But I never quit!!!

DRILL TOWER 40

After Drill Tower 89, we were sent to San Pedro to Drill Tower 40. This was where we were taught hose evolutions. There is an art to pulling hose. It looks like a beautiful dance when it's done correctly. Someone was always behind you helping you get the nozzle to the imagined fire. Every evolution flowed, with us all doing our part. You always knew when someone messed up because the timing would be off. Attaching a supply hose to a hydrant and pumping water to the fire was also taught in its basic form. I was in class all by myself! All the other girls had fizzled out. It was just me…the only woman, training with ex-football and baseball players. It seemed every day the instructors were trying to think up new ways to eliminate me.

They finally got their chance when during one of the long hose evolutions to get to an imagined faraway fire, I stopped during the hose-lay. When my load got too heavy…I stopped to look back; wondering where my help was? The captain yelled at me to get back to work, getting the hose to the imagined fire. I told him I was waiting for my help, but he told me, "There is no help! You are all alone." I dropped the hose where I was and backtracked to get a coupling to advance the hose, the same way I would have if I had help.

The next day our training scheduling was changed to a hose drag that was connected to a four-way hydrant valve. They used the two strongest guys in our class and told them that after they went up and over, instead of lining up as they usually did to pick up the four-way valve that was attached to two hundred feet of three-and-half-inch hose and drag it about two hundred feet. A line was drawn on the ground to mark our goal. Then they were told to pull all the hose over the line. This proved to be too difficult for our strongest guys, so they modified it while we stood at attention and watched. One of the guys standing next to me asked, "Why are they making us do this? No other class had to do this!"

I said, "Because of me. We are doing this for me." One by one we watched as others took their turn and pulled that hose. I was last to go…and the guys who were in front of me wondered if I could pass this new test. I was angry and tired of always being in the spotlight, but it was finally my turn! I took off at a sprint for about a hundred feet and then the weight just stopped me in my tracks! I felt as if I had been yanked back! I looked behind me at the line of hose left to drag forward, and how far I had to go, and wanted to give up then and there! That's when my classmates started to chant my last name in low voices…."Come on, Lasley. Come on, Lasley." I took a step with each chant. I felt like I was perpendicular to the ground, but the weight of the hose kept me from falling face forward to the asphalt. I gained ground with each chant as it got louder and louder! I finally made it to the finish line looking like The Hunchback, only able to take one dragging step at a time! Exhausted at the line, yet I still had to pull the hose over the marker, and behind me to complete the task. It was the most difficult task I faced, but thanks to the guys cheering me on, I accomplished it!!

Thank you for teaching me kindness in teamwork I knew one of the instructors didn't want me to be successful. I had a job waiting for me at Kaiser. Kaiser had called me back after the lay-offs. Why was I putting myself through this? I knew it was always going to be like this! Someone always thinking I couldn't do this job and letting me know I didn't belong. I didn't have to take this shit! I went home and told my mother, "I'm quitting the Fire Department, and I'm going back to work at Kaiser!"

She said, "Okay, if that's what you want to do… but if you let them run you away, what will you say to your sons if they ever want to become firefighters when they grow up? Make them fire you! Don't give them your career because that's what it is, Kay. It's a career, not a job! The Fire Department doesn't lay people off."

I returned with a prayer that GOD would help me show them all what I was capable of, and a calm spirit came over me as I sat outside the gates of D.T. 40, waiting for the place to open up.

I was being singled out and persecuted because of my gender. They came up with another way to get me out, using the written test we took every day. I knew I was given a different test than the others because after the testing was over, and we were waiting for everyone else to finish, we would ask each other, "What did you get for number such and such?" The guys would start memorizing some of the questions to compare answers. I knew some of the questions were changed on my test, worded differently. No way would I get it wrong. I studied long before I arrived to the drill tower. I started studying when I was a pre-trainee, back at Westlake. I studied the rules and regulations as well as the fire prevention volumes. I knew this stuff!

One day after failing an easy test and understanding that my test had been slightly altered, two others along with me were called into the captain's office. The captain went around the room telling the guys what they need to work on. When he came to me, he said, "And Karen, I'm really surprised at you!"

I looked him straight in the eye, and said, "I'm just as surprised as you, sir." He knew that I knew…. And I got the same test as the others in class after saying this! Whenever one of us recruits was the best at something, the peer-group instructors would make a big deal out of it. The instructors would announce the top scores of the day to build esteem and confidence and make recruits feel like they were the best in the class. This developed healthy competition. It made us feel like we were on top of the world.

I was the fastest in donning my breathing apparatus while reciting all the components of it. No one mentioned it until at the end of the day. When one of the guys asked when we were in class after taking a written test, "Hey, Captain, who had the fastest time donning the B.A.?" He replied, "Karen." That's all…just my name. This was another person who didn't want me in the fire department. He took joy in making me miserable. On our last day at Drill Tower 40, we were all so happy to have passed another milestone. As we lined up to shake all of our drill instructors' hands, I came to the one who had given me such a hard time…I refused to look him in the eye…I was just going through the motions of politeness. I didn't want to touch him, and he knew it! I tried to get by him as quickly as possible, but he gripped my hand tight and willed me to see him. I looked up with hostility in my eyes and saw RESPECT FOR ME IN HIS... I won him over by not quitting. Thank you for teaching me perseverance.

CHAPTER *18*

Back to Drill Tower 89

It had been reported to the Board of Fire Commissioners that three of the members of our class were weak and termination was in their near future, so they came out on our first day back at D.T. 89 to see for themselves. I was one of the three our board was looking at closely. Our evaluation started with us lifting ladders. Just the three of us. I was a little rusty on technique but clearly had no strength problem. The other two guys were so rattled by this new development of being in the spotlight they made me look good. It was a lot of pressure on them being in the same class with me. Nothing new to me; it was business as usual.

Next came the dreaded UP AND OVER! BUT INSTEAD OF DOING IT TWICE, WE DID IT THREE TIMES!!! This included the whole class of recruits. This was an old battle from Westlake Training that I thought was over. One of the captains in charge at Westlake was now in charge of us in the drill tower. And he made it clear to me he was opposed to women being in the department! Captain R. said to us, as we came down to line up the third time, as we were bending over trying to catch our breath, "Stand up straight!" I stood up and looked him straight in the eyes. He had an evil smile on his face! He looked at one of my classmates and said his name, ordering him to stand up straight. I looked back at my classmate, one of our strongest… as he turned green trying to stand up straight.

I told the captain, "You better catch him." As my classmate started to crumble in a faint, I went into nurse mode, ordering someone to get the oxygen (The Elder) while I broke formation to get wet paper towels to cool my classmate's body temperature. Someone else ran to get the paramedics, who were close by in the Task Force House at F.S. #89. When they arrived, I had O2 started, and my classmate was coming around. As the paramedics assessed him, they asked, "Why is he wet?"

I told them, "I used cold water to cool him down." They praised my first aid, and my classmate told me the cool water is what woke him up; it was refreshing. All these things occurred in front of the fire commissioners who were present to witness my shortcomings and approve termination. After PT was over, I was summoned to the chief's office...Chief Orduna wanted to see me! This was a scary meeting because he was the most powerful person next to the board when it came to my continuing at the training academy. He was also the highest-ranking Black man in the fire department. We were proud of him as a representative of the Black race, and I wanted his respect. It was an honor to be noticed by him. As I stood at attention, he smiled at me and told me he had been following my progress and wanted me to do better going up and over. He wanted me to stop being the last one all the time. I said, "Sir, I hate going up and over, and I can't be good at something I hate! I've gotten better, but so have the guys in my class. I can't promise you I will not be last, but I will promise you I won't quit! "But you need to understand I may always be the last one because I hate it!" He said, "Just don't quit." And after our meeting, he told everyone who was giving me a hard time to leave me alone!

CHAPTER 19

Jump for Your Job

Now it came down to who's afraid of heights? The tried and true way to test us in this area was by making us rappel down the side of the six-story building we scaled every workday. It was fun to me. The hard part was getting your weight off the rope to unlock the carabiner. You had to pull up with one hand while releasing with the other. Not an easy task for people with no upper body strength, but it was fun.

Jumping into a Life-net was also required. We jumped out of a three-story window into the life net being held by our classmates, who were just as new as us in this area. It took trust in the equipment as well as each other. I didn't like it! Not having control. As long as I could hold on to something, I was okay, but letting go and jumping feet first, then making sure to rotate on your back made me uneasy. Just the thought of it! The guys knew I was hesitant, and the instructors played a mind game with me when my turn came. They told me to look out and into the apartment in the distance; there was a nude man standing there. Then they said, "Jump!"

It seemed like I was falling forever. Just when I started to scream, I hit the net! They heard the squeak just before I hit the canvas and teased me about it. The airbag was a piece of cake. Anyone who refused to jump was disqualified. Captain R. found a weakness and just before we graduated he wrote me up saying I was afraid of heights! I would sign my career away if I marked that I concurred. I looked at him as if to say YOU JUST WON'T STOP, WILL YOU? I checked I do not concur! Later that day I was called into the Captain II office, and Captain R. was there also. The Captain II told me that Captain R. wanted me to sign something. It was the same write-up about me being afraid of heights! I told him, "This is the same write-up as before!"

He said in an exasperated voice, "Well, Karen, if you do not concur, check that you do not concur!" I checked the box that said, I DO NOT CONCUR while saying it out loud to him! They told me later no trainee had ever checked that box before; they always went along with the program and signed their job away.

EXIT INTERVIEW

The day before graduation we met with all the staff of the Drill Academy, and they asked me what they could do to make women more successful in passing the drill tower. I said, "Maybe I passed because I have something to push me and that's my kids… I'm basically a shy person and being in the spotlight is hard for me. I never got a break when the guys took one because someone was always watching me."

Captain R. said, "Nobody was watching you; it was just your imagination." I clammed up and refused to continue with the exit interview until one of the other captains said, "It's true we do look for you when you are out on the yard. You stand out. Everything about you stands out. The way you look and walk draws our eyes to you. And your voice calling 'All clear' is new to us. And it's something you're going to have to get used to." I thanked him for being honest with me.

CHAPTER 20

Graduation Day

THIS IS THE DAY WE ALL HAVE BEEN WAITING FOR! We did it, and nothing about it was easy. Now it was time to show all our supporters how their help paid off. We were putting on a show for our family and friends, doing what firefighters do. We laid out hose and fought fire in a ballet of organization and skill while rescuing class mates from the third floor of the building we jumped from during training. After the show was over, we lined up in our dress uniforms and took our oaths. I waited for my name to be called and although I only had a few people in the audience—my mother, sister Pam, Aunt Linda and two sons Aaron and Brandon—the thunderous clapping came from people I didn't know, but who knew my story. As hats were thrown in the air, I thought of all the times I wanted to quit and the hurdles I had to overcome. I knew there was nothing I couldn't do as long as I tried with everything inside me. As a reminder of this day, my mother gave me a pair of diamond stud earrings. Thank you for teaching me with God on my side I can do anything.

The Firefighters Oath
When I am called to duty, God, wherever flames may rage, give me strength to save some life, whatever be its age. Help me embrace a little child before it is too late or save an older person, from the horror of that fate. Enable me to be alert and hear the weakest shout, quickly and efficiently to put the

fire out. I want to fill my calling to give the best in me to guard my every neighbor and protect his property. And if, according to my fate, I am to lose my life, please bless with your protecting hand my children and my everlasting life.

Amen

CHAPTER 21

Aaron's Perspective, A Past Event that Changed My Life

Damn, it's hot! I don't think I was ever hotter. Boy, the heat. As I sat outside with the rest of my family, the heat began to cause my suit, or dress clothes as we call them in the Hood, to become my own portable sauna. Although the heat wasn't the half of it! The stirring voices and the anxious family and friends became overwhelming. The cheap little fold-out chair was becoming hot, but I didn't pay it any mind. The time was growing near, and the constant movement I made caused my grandmother to pop me on my leg and push me back in my seat. The cool breeze that came once every twenty minutes was like a young mother rubbing her child's pain away and slowly caused the anxiety to fade within me. That's when I saw her. She stood tall and strong, and at this moment, I knew a drastic change was going to overwhelm us. She stood strong. As if she were a lioness, standing after a hard kill, with her chest out and eyes straight. It was the most magnificent thing I have ever seen. At that moment I was looking at my biggest hero or heroine. This woman went against the odds and succeeded. Although her skin was brown, she shined as bright as the sun. She shined the brightest out of all those who stood beside her. She became so much more than what I saw in that little fold-out seat of mine. She became an example of dedication, hope, and love. She achieved her goal, and at that moment sparked a fire in me that could warm the earth itself. I was proud! As one lonely tear ran down my cheek, I understood that no one could hold me or stop me. I stood for hope, love, and all that I value. I stood up to congratulate the one who conceived and protected me, My Friend, My Homie, My Pal. The one who would be there forever, my mother. I loved her then, and I love her now.

At this moment the clouds in the sky cracked open, allowing a beam of light to embrace her. Now that I think about it, after a while I wasn't so hot anymore. As I looked and read the story her eyes told, I sympathized. Another lonely tear rolled down, and the breeze blew it away along with my sadness. I sat up straight and watched as hats took flight, like a flock of birds taking off, just to return in a matter of seconds.

CONGRATULATIONS, MOM! I love you—from the little boy in the third row in the seventh seat.

By AARON EUGENE LASLEY
THANK YOU, AARON (VON RUBINSTINE)

CHAPTER 22

My First House Fire
Station #35 Task-Force

My first house was my truck house, and all my supporters thought they were again setting me up for failure. The year of probation is spent working at three fire stations: two engine houses and one truck house. The truck house is where you learn all the tools and equipment. To prove you know everything, you have to give drills in the morning after line-up. The drill involves you telling the entire crew how to use a piece of equipment. You also need to describe the safety and maintenance of the object. The guys ask you questions when you finish the drill, and this is when you learn everything you need to know that's not in the books. The guys always showed you something new. If they wanted to get you, they could make you look bad in front of the captain by asking you things they knew you wouldn't know. The truck was stuffed with everything you can imagine for building and destroying. Depending on the building, depending on the need. I had to learn where everything was stored as well as how to use, clean and maintain every piece of equipment stored on the truck. Not an easy task while running calls all day. Fire Station #35 was a busy fire station with eager firefighters, young and old. Pride was evident in the way the apparatus and station were maintained. The place shone.

FIRE STATION 35

My first task was to learn all the inventory on the truck and its use. I was so tired at the end of the day and knew the guys working with me were also. I felt bad asking them to help me when they were relaxing in the TV room. So instead of asking for help, I came back on my off days to take pictures and learn as much as I could, using the other rookies and picking the brains of everyone I knew who had finished their truck house before me. I had it down! I thought....On the day of my truck inventory exam, I opened the first compartment and turned my back on it, then started to rattle off everything that was stored inside. As I proceeded to the next compartment, one of the guys asked me a question that I didn't know the answer to. As I opened the next door to tell them what was inside, I was hit with another question I had no answer for. I couldn't get over the fact that I was missing information as the guys started their rapid-fire questions. And I started spinning in confusion. It was so bad, I forgot the things I did know. The more I found out I didn't know, the wider my smile became as I answered them with an "I don't know." Over and over again...I wanted to crawl in a hole and cry. But all they saw was my smile.

My Captain II put a stop to my misery, calling me into the front office. He said, "Karen, I don't think you are taking this seriously. Why didn't you prepare? The guys heard you came on your off days to learn the inventory. Who helped you?" I said, "I asked the rookies on the other shifts and a friend of mine who finished his truck house to help me." All the while I had a huge smile on my face. He said, "Why are you smiling? This is no joke!"

I said, "Just because I'm smiling doesn't mean I'm happy... just the opposite. I've had a friend come up to me and say their mother died and I smiled as I said, 'I'm so sorry to hear that.' I smile to keep from crying." (My tears start to flow.) I told him, "I didn't want to bother the guys on my shift because I know how tired they are after running calls all day because I'm tired too. That's why I came on my off days."

He said, "They were punishing you because they heard what you did. No one can teach you about the Truck better than them, they were insulted!" He didn't expect me to know the answers to some of those questions. He understood me better, and from then on and someone was assigned to me every day to help me with my drills. The guys took pride in my growth, and my monthly reviews were always very good. The evaluation was rated from one to four with the four being the highest rating you could receive, and I was well into the fours. When our battalion chief heard I was getting fours, he called my captain and told him he was coming over to see for himself. They laid out fire hose and rope for a knot drill as well as tools and equipment for me to demonstrate my knowledge on.

The guys were pissed-off with the chief for thinking they were giving me a pass because I was a woman. I had my game face on, smile firmly in place. The bigger my smile got, the kinder my guys were to me as I answered this new challenge. They knew I was nervous and reassured me with each drill that I was doing great. When it came to the knot drill, after tying each one, the chief asked what the name of the knot was and how would it is used. I mistakenly told him one of the knots was a bowline away. Then I looked up and saw one of my firefighters running in the doorway of the apparatus floor bathroom and realized my mistake. I said, "Pardon me, sir, that's a running bowline, not a bowline away."

The chief saw Mike, the firefighter running in place to give me a clue and realized the guys were all loyal to me. I was asked to put the rotary saw in the outboard position. I did it with little effort. The chief then asked me to adjust the belt; the firefighter who was assigned to help me learn this tool stepped up and said, "Chief, I didn't teach her how to do that yet."

I said, "I read about it and know what to do." I turned the screw as I hung the blade off the tailboard, and it lifted in the perfect position to show it was balanced just like the training book said it would do. After everything was over and the chief left the station, the captain called line-up and told the guys the chief said, "You're right, she does deserve fours, not only for knowing all her drills but for winning the respect of all of her peers." That felt good.

At night before we all fell asleep in our dorm room, I would tell the guys stories about strong women. I told them stories I read in my romance novels, and I would always leave them hanging for the next part of the adventure. If they treated me mean throughout the day, I would refuse to tell them the rest of the story as we fell asleep.

They knew I had a soft heart and was naive to the ugliness of the world. We moved up to cover for another fire station in downtown Los Angeles. As we pulled inside the station, I saw a man lying down on the ground across the street with bags spilled around him. I thought he was ill and asked if we should check on him. They laughed at me and said, "Go ahead, rookie, and check on him… yourself." I didn't go, but I did watch him from the front window until we were cleared to go back home to our fire station.

That night as I finally started falling asleep, after tossing and turning, one the firefighters said, "I can't sleep. I keep thinking about the poor bastard the rookie left on the street to die!" **EVERYONE IN THE DORM STARTED TO LAUGH OUT LOUD!** They knew I was the one having a hard time sleeping and let me know in their own way that the drunk was okay.

It was hard leaving my first house. But on my last night I got revenge on one of my hard cases. I put graphite all around his helmet liner. I wasn't there to see the black line it left on his forehead when he took his helmet off, but I know they knew it was me. They used to play all kinds of tricks on each other and being a rookie, I was fair game. I had to answer the phone when it rang and someone was always racing me to it. They were not supposed to be able to beat me to it! One day we were eating when the phone rang and after answering it, I went back to the table and sat down. One of the guys had spilled a puddle of water for me to sit in. I looked like I wet myself and was not happy about it… I knew who did it! It was the guy who had received the phone call. I asked the engineer sitting across from me at the table if rookies were allowed to get people back. He said yes. When the firefighter came back after his phone call, a puddle of water was waiting for him. He looked at me and said, "I know the rookie didn't do this!"

I said, "Do what?" Everyone laughed because I looked so innocent. He didn't know who got him...until I was transferred to my new assignment and the graphite incident was discovered.

I took at least three showers a day working at Fire Station 35, one in the morning, one after exercise, and if we had a fire, I took another one. If there was no fire call, I took one at bedtime. They finally noticed my habits and said to me, "Karen, you don't like getting dirty, do you?"

I said, "I don't mind getting dirty as long as I can get clean." The truth was, it was my only escape from them. Don't get me wrong they were very good to me. It was like having big brothers always around... I needed alone time.

They couldn't follow me in the shower, and no one wanted to water the small patch of grass in front of the station, so I had two places to escape from them.

CHAPTER 23

Chitterlings

On my last shift working at Fire Station 35, I was required to show my appreciation by cooking a great meal. My captain had heard I gave another captain some chitterlings when I was in the drill tower and asked me to make them some. I asked, him, "Do you know what chitterlings are?"

He said, "No."

I told him, "You don't want chitterlings."

He said, "Yes, we do. We heard how good they are. What are chitterlings?" I refused to tell him. I told him he didn't want any… but he insisted. Only two other people in the station knew what chitterlings were, and one of them refused to eat them but promised he would not tell the guys what they were made from until they tasted them. I also cooked black-eyed peas, coleslaw, and cornbread, and I made a pot roast for the ones who refused to eat chitterlings. I fixed everyone's plate and waited for everyone to start eating…and guessing….

One guy said, "How did you skin the chicken?"

I said, with a big smile, "It's not chicken; its pig intestines." I had to repeat myself several times. They didn't believe me until the firefighter who didn't eat chitterlings told them I was telling the truth. **THEY ALL STARTED SPITTING THEIR FOOD OUT!**

It's a good thing I also made the pot roast. I took my chitterlings back home where I prepared them and cooked them. They have their own smell and it would have been obvious if I had cooked them at the station. Back home they were appreciated.

FIRE STATION 52

At my second house as a rookie, my regular captain was out on an injury long term. The captain who replaced him was the same one who did my background interview when I was trying to get on the job. He was an asshole! He refused to pass me the first time for unknown reasons. Maybe it was because I smoked weed in the 12th grade or because I filed bankruptcy after my divorce from Calvin. He had no real answer when I asked him why. I had to speak to his captain before I found out he had no valid reason for disqualifying me. I was told to simply reapply. He was not happy to see me progress to the next level and made it known when we met at Fire Station 52.

He was another one of those who thought up drills to test me every day…Thank GOD, I had an engineer who was looking out for me until our regular captain came back to duty. Old Fire Station 52 had a separate building for the kitchen. It was located in the backyard, outside the apparatus floor doors. The apparatus floor, the office, the dorm room and bathroom were in the main building. Back in the day, the fire department used horses to get to the fires. These old fire stations had barns for horses. Our kitchen was in that barn's converted space. One night I was in the kitchen studying. The captain left his briefcase open on the kitchen table when he went inside the front office building. I had my back to the T.V. because we, as rookies on probation, were not allowed to watch it. All of a sudden the captain burst open the door, looked at his briefcase and then me…like I was going through it! I looked at him and shook my head as if to say, shame on you for thinking I'm a thief! His attitude was a little better after this encounter but not much…When my regular captain came back, this captain gave me glowing reviews. But I was glad he was finally gone. My real captain was nothing like him. Fire Station 52 was my first engine house of another three-month probation period until the final station. I didn't cook chitterlings for them when I left... I cooked them food they had already been introduced to.

CHAPTER 24

Fire Station 82

My third and final house! This was to be my home from now on…if I passed probation. My captain was a very good-looking Italian man with a house full of kids. His wife was as beautiful as he was, inside and out. This is where I became certified on driving the engine. Fire Station 82 is the storage house for the reserve apparatus. Whenever a rig broke down in the City of Los Angeles, Fire Station 82 is where they came to switch over until their rig was fixed. On Monday, we had to do safety and mechanical checks on all the reserve apparatus. It was added work for us, but the tradeoff is we learned about all kinds of pumpers. Some had open cabs. I learned to drive this kind first.

My captain taught us to drive by the spanner method! Riding in an open cab, everyone must wear a helmet. A spanner is a long handle brass tool used to turn on the water from the fire hydrant. Driving by spanner method meant every time I missed a gear while shifting, my captain would hit me on the helmet with it! It was a startling experience! After about the third time of being hit on the head with that thing, I stopped the rig in the middle of the street and said, "The next time you hit me with that thing, I'm going to wreck this rig!" That was the end of my spanner training.

My captain took on a fatherly role entirely on his own. He thought I needed guidance in the dating area. I was newly divorced and having a great time. I learned early on in the dating game not to give my phone number out to strangers. Not until got to know them better. And I learned the hard way…it was difficult to get rid of the undesirable ones. After I learned my lesson, I decided I would be a better idea to let the guys come to the fire station. I could feel them out there. But it never failed; if we were in the front office, my captain would be in the front office. If we were in the kitchen, my captain would be in the kitchen. If I gave my captain the sign to leave us alone, he would cross his arms in front of his body to signal NO!

He followed us to every room we moved to and pretended he needed to be there too. After my date would leave, my captain would say, "Get rid of him; he's no good for you! And 99 percent of the time he was right! He approved only one guy, and I married him… Michael. (Michael Roger Slider the man of my dreams.) The day we were getting a new battalion chief, and our captain had heard this new chief was a hard man to please. He was worried about him being too tough on us. The chief was known to be hard on crews on incident runs. Our captain told all of us to be on our toes when the new chief came to meet us. Wendy (a paramedic) and I, the only women on our shift, were in the kitchen cooking lunch when the chief arrived to meet us. We had our back to him as he entered. He noticed we had our boots off, showing our bare feet. As we turned around, he saw our shirts were stuffed with pillows to make us look like we were pregnant. Wendy said, "Hello, sir, it's nice to meet you, but you should know we are only allowed to be here if we are barefoot and pregnant!" Our captain looked like he was in shock! THEY LAUGHED!! It broke the ice, and our new chief loved Fire Station 82, us.

We had a single-family structure fire soon after I arrived at Fire Station 82 and the single-family house was well involved in fire, when we arrived. My assignment was to protect the house next door from the fire. I was instructed to put a two-and-a-half-inch hose line into operation. As I advanced the hose to the back of the structure, I encountered a locked fence with an RV parked in front of it. It was in the way of my advancing the hose and I went back to the fire engine to tell my captain I couldn't advance the line. He looked at me like I had lost my mind and said, "I don't care what you have to do! But you better get your ass over that fence and put that line into operation!"

I went back and climbed the fence with the line wrapped around me. By the time the other companies arrived, we were all in place putting the fire out and protecting exposures. The chief looked at me sitting on the two-and-a-half-inch line like I was the best thing since sliced bread. He had no idea what it took for my captain to get me there, in that position, to protect the exposure. When we got back to the station, I was called into the front office, and my captain said, "Firefighters are called when there is no one else to call! And we don't quit. We don't stop until the work is done, or we are relieved of duty." I never forgot that lesson and passed it down to rookies along the way.

CHAPTER 25

Intuition

Late one night we got a run for a person down. When we turned the corner to the address, I got an eerie feeling. All the streetlights were off; it was dark. and everything was too quiet. We had the rescue ambulance with us, but I felt like something bad would happen if we separated.

I kept insisting the guys stay together. If I saw one of us go in a different direction, away from us, I would say, "Don't go over there by yourself," or I'd say, "Come back and stay with us." It ended up being a false alarm. When we got back to the station, my captain asked me why I was so adamant we all stay together. I told him I had a bad feeling when we turned the corner. He understood. He said he would always listen to me. Whenever I felt something was wrong to tell him because he had felt the same kind of warning signs, he listened, and it saved lives.

He told me a story. He said, "One night we had a fire in an abandoned warehouse. All the windows had bars on them. I felt the same way as you, that something bad would happen if we went inside before the windows were opened up. All the firefighters who showed up wanted to go in through the front door. But I held them in place while the fire grew. When the bars were cut off and the windows opened up, we advanced to the fire and noticed it was an arson fire and there were traps in place to kill us. If I had not listened to my inner voice, someone would have died. I couldn't explain it, but I knew I had to hold everyone at the door until all the bars were removed. Intuition never lets you down."

FIRE STATION 66

I had to grow in the fire service… Fire Station 82 was home for me, but I wanted to learn more and be promoted one day to battalion chief. My captain told me he would retire before he let me be a higher rank than him. It was hard leaving, but I knew it was time. I had learned all I could working Hollywood as a firefighter.

When I arrived at Fire Station 66, I was not welcomed by the other firefighters. It seemed I was always going to have to earn respect. I did my job, but it was never enough to get the respect I was due. They let me know by the way they talked and acted. Some of them refused to eat when I cooked. Sometimes they would make a plate of food and put on a show by spitting out the food on their plate and then throwing the rest away. One of the guys who was eating said of the person who spit his food out, "I didn't know he was so picky about what he eats…" Letting me know the guy was an asshole and my food was good. The assholes would ask, "Karen, do you like watermelon?" I would reply, "I love watermelon, don't you?"

CHAPTER 26

Arnett Hartsfield

The treatment I was receiving soon got around to my staunch supporters, and they showed up at the fire station, one by one, to give me words of encouragement. I needed to stand up for myself. I was no longer on probation. I wasn't even a Boot at this station. The first supporter to show up was Mr. Arnett Hartsfield, Jr. He was the man. He was responsible for affirmative action being taking seriously during the 1960s. He even wrote a book about his days as a Black firefighter in an all-white fire station. I had no idea who he was when one of the guys found me and said, "Mr. Hartsfield is here to see you."

He was a slim, light-skinned Black man with a ready smile on his face. As I approached him and held out my hand for a shake, he embraced me in a warm hug and said, "You don't know who I am, but I know all about you." He started telling me all about my trials and tribulations, from the drill tower to my present assignment at Fire Station 66. He knew everything I endured and was proud of me. He was active in the affirmative action goals and the retention of women was his next goal. I loved him and knew he felt the same way about me. In an endearing way, a fatherly way…

The secretary of the Head of the Board of Fire Commissioners (Eva Whitelock) was the next person to show up in my support. She was a feared presence. The first Black female firefighter, Da Lisa D., showed up soon after. This left no doubt in the crew's minds as to how many important people were looking out for me, and they soon backed off. My supporters gave me permission to be me. From this point on, I let my voice be heard. It seemed that Fire Station 66 was filled with people who had no idea who they were serving. Most of the crew was made up of white men, but the area they served was made up with low-income Black people. The attitude was very poor on the Fireside.

One night we were called for a man running nude on the street. When we arrived, we noticed steam radiating from his body. It was a very cold night. This was a sure sign of PCP intoxication. He was respectful but clear when he refused to let the guys touch him. They were joking among themselves about his condition. I approached him and asked if he would let me take his vital signs. He said, "Yes, you can. I know they don't care about me! Only you can touch me, not them."

He was so right. I could see it too; they thought it was beneath them to touch him. After the patient was transferred into the care of the paramedics, I let all of my coworkers know how I felt. I said, "If I ever see you all treat an altered patient that way again, I will file a complaint against you all!" I saw the way they treated the few white people who they thought were stuck in the District. They would bend over backward for them.

But the poor Black people living in the District were treated like they were the lowest forms of humanity, and I was not going to let them treat people that way while I was around. I said, "From now on everyone gets the same treatment or I'm telling! That's how my mother raised me." Thank you for teaching me to love people, the way I want to be loved, Mom.

BRUSH CLEARANCE UNIT

My assignment at Fire Station 66 ended after a traffic accident that resulted in my back being injured. While responding to a run on the EMT (800) ambulance, we were hit in the rear right passenger side cab by a pickup truck. This is how I ended up on light duty, in the Brush Clearance Unit of the Fire Prevention Bureau. My assignment entailed dealing with public complaints. I learned a lot working there. When I was once again fit for full duty, I was transferred to Fire Station 99.

CHAPTER 27

Fire Station 99

This fire station was in Los Angeles, with a Beverly Hills zip code, 90210. It was located on the top of the hill of Beverly Glen and Mulholland. The homes of the rich and famous! Although our emergency runs were few, when we did go out on a call, it was an experience. The area was dense with brush and curved streets. If you didn't know the streets, it was easy to get lost. I can't tell you how many times the police drove around us in circles, trying to respond to our location. We would hear their sirens all around us, circling.

We learned to rely on the other fire stations on the Hill, Fire Stations 109 and 108. They were on the opposite sides of us, on Mulholland Drive, bordering our district but always responded to our incident if we needed help before LAPD could find our location. Our district was so complex, only one fire station at a time was allowed to go off the Hill, as we called it, to shop for food. Long ago, some rich person's house burned down because the responding units were unable to get there, fast enough. All the fire stations on the hill, 99, 109, and 108, were shopping at once and the move-up companies got lost or were too far away to get to the incident in time to save the structure. Million-dollar homes and contents to match. This was unacceptable, so we had to ask permission from our dispatch to shop every day for dinner. We all took turns cooking. Every firefighter knows how to cook at least one good meal. I ended up being the permanent cook at Fire Station 99.

It was easy for me. I've been cooking since I was nine for my brothers and sisters. My mother worked and put Pam and me in charge of cleaning and cooking. She would call us on the telephone and give us instructions and check on us by phone throughout the day to make sure everything was on schedule. I love to cook. I love the look on everyone's face when everything is cooked to perfection. The only problem is after I finish cooking, I'm rarely hungry. Something about smelling the food and tasting it while I'm preparing it takes my appetite away.

CHAPTER 28

Riots

I was working at Fire Station 99 when the riots broke out, in March 1991. Rodney King was a Black man who was beaten after running from the police in a car chase. The car chase was caught on camera for the whole world to see. It was the last straw for Black people! We knew what was going to happen to Rodney King when we watched it unfold on TV. We had been living with these consequences our whole life. You don't run from the police and get caught without an ass-whipping!

The Hispanic people seeing Rodney get his beatdown were not surprised either! But all the people I worked with, mostly white men living in the suburbs of Los Angeles County, were caught off guard. They started saying things like, "This is wrong! I didn't know the police treated Black people this way!" It seemed to be the common thought process of a lot of white people who saw it on TV, and I started thinking... Wow! Things are going to change for the Black man now that the whole world knows! I went to work every shift thinking at last my sons won't have to live in fear of the police like so many of my family and friends did as I grew up. But after watching the trial of the police officers in Simi Valley, a predominately white community, it was plain to see nothing was going to change for the Black people who held out hope just yet...

Psalm 45

My heart is stirred by a noble theme,
as I sing my ode to the king.
My tongue is the pen of a nimble scribe.

Psalm 45

You are the most handsome of men;
Fair speech has graced your lips,
For God has blessed you forever.
Gird your sword upon your hip, mighty warrior!
In splendor and majesty ride on triumphant!
In the cause of truth, meekness, and justice
May your right hand show your wondrous deeds.
Your arrows are sharp;
Peoples will cower at your feet;
The king's enemies will lose heart.
Your throne, O God,* stands forever;
Your royal scepter is a scepter for justice.
You love justice and hate wrongdoing;
Therefore God, your God, has anointed you
With the oil of gladness above your fellow kings.
With myrrh, aloes, and cassia
Your robes are fragrant.
From ivory-paneled palaces
Stringed instruments bring you joy.
Daughters of kings are your lovely wives;
A princess arrayed in Ophir's gold
Comes to stand at your right hand.

Listen, my daughter, and understand;
Pay me careful heed.
Forget your people and your father's house,
That the king might desire your beauty.
He is your lord;

Honor him, daughter of Tyre.
Then the richest of the people
Will seek your favor with gifts.
All glorious is the king's daughter as she enters,
Her raiment threaded with gold;
In embroidered apparel she is led to the king.
The maids of her train are presented to the king.
They are led in with glad and joyous acclaim;
They enter the palace of the king.

The throne of your fathers your sons will have;
You shall make them princes through all the land.
I will make your name renowned through all generations;
Thus, nations shall praise you forever.

I tried to explain to my coworkers why we, as Black people, were so upset, but they started seeing this injustice as an issue the police department was better able to handle. On the day the police officers were found NOT GUILTY!!! I knew all hell was about to break loose! Everyone I knew was talking about how things were finally going to change. Now it was like an April Fool's joke. I tried to warn everyone at work to take a nap because it was going to be a long night! No one paid me any attention. I went to the dorm to heed my own advice and get some rest before the storm.

When I awoke, my best friend, Marsha, who worked across the street from LAPD headquarters, called to tell me, "Hey, girl, they are storming Parker Center!" I told her to hold on as I announced it over the loudspeaker to the guys, who were still watching the trial updates on television. I said, "Hey, guys, I told you to take a nap; now they're storming Parker Center."

They laughed at me and said, "No, they're not! It would be on the news if they were storming Parker Center!" No sooner had these words left their mouths than "Breaking News" reported what I was saying to them over the loudspeaker.

Marsha lived on 118th street. On her way home from work, she passed the riots, starting on Normandy and Florence. Again, she called me when she got home to report what was happening in South Central Los Angeles. You would have thought I was in charge of the looting, riots, and chaos by the way my co-workers looked at me every time I conveyed to them how bad things were getting as the day progressed. I was sitting in the TV room, watching everything unfold, feeling the pain of all those who were rebelling, knowing it was all a reflection of times past. I thought of the riots of the 1960s that took so many lives. I thought of the neighborhood mom and pop stores we lost back then. All of the nice Jewish people who gave my mother credit on just her word to pay them back on the first or fifteenth. (The first and the fifteenth of every month was when she got her welfare check.)

It was both exciting and sad at the same time. I knew change was necessary but at what cost? I felt like I was no longer one of them…a fellow firefighter. They saw me as one of the rioters, on the side of the unruly Black people, who were pulling innocent truck drivers out of their trucks and beating them senseless, just because they happened to be in the wrong place at the wrong time. The people I worked with lived in a different world than I. They could not understand how we as Black people felt every day. How could they? They thought what happened to Rodney King was unjust until they watched the trial on the TV. I warned them Black people were sick and tired of the abuse. All of us, the Black people I knew were thinking, now the world knows how Black People are treated by the police! A change is coming! It was a slap in the face when the verdict came out and the police officers were cleared of any and all wrongdoing.

Engine 99 was called off the Hill to move up to the command post and base. Fires were being set all over the city of Los Angeles. We, firefighters and police officers, never had a moment's rest. As we put out one fire, another was set in its place. I have never been so tired in my life! To make matters worse, the rioters were shooting at police officers, and my husband, Michael, was out there somewhere doing his job. I had no way of contacting him, nor him me. All my family who lived in the danger zone drove to the Valley to our home to be with my mother. My niece Khristina told my sister Pamala, "If we are going to die, I want to die with Grandma!" They felt safe with her. As the night grew late and we as an engine company had made no progress in firefighting due to the anger of the rioters, I was in a store getting drinks and chips to fuel our tired bodies when a young Black man asked me, "HOW YOU LIKE YOUR JOB NOW!?"

I said, "I don't, and I wish you all would just stop!" We were putting out a fire in a strip mall as people were running inside a shoe store next to the store on fire, looting. Then I noticed a homeless man with a shopping cart picking up cans in the parking lot. He looked at me and shook his head in shame at the looters. If anyone had a need, he did, yet his morals were still intact. He might be down on his luck, but he was no thief.

WE FOUGHT FIRE WELL INTO THE EARLY MORNING! If it weren't for the leftover Easter candy the public provided, we would have run out of energy long before we did. There was no place open to buy food. And we never made it to base or were relieved of duty by another company. We just kept breaking down our hose line to fuel our rig before we ran out. Then we were released to go home—or I should say we just went back to our station when we realized they had lost us in the shuffle of resources.

The next day at home, I slept the whole day and night away, and so did my police officer husband. I have never been that tired in my life! When it was time to return to work after the riots, things were not the same. I was informed it would be better if we all took turns cooking. They no longer wanted me to be the permanent cook. Which was cool with me. I no longer wanted to cook for them. They let me know how they felt during the civil unrest. I was considered one of the Black people who were in agreement with the rioters. In their eyes, that meant I was against them...

My fellow firefighters felt like they were in danger for just being white men. Many of them enrolled in self-defense classes. Some took up karate to become black belts. Guns were not allowed on fire department property, so they tried to protect themselves as best they could. It was strange to me. I was hurt because I thought I could tell them anything…I found out that was a big mistake. They were secure in the world they lived in. The truth made them feel insecure.

Dr. Boxley, the department psychologist, was called in to help mend the divide between us and other fire stations, who were experiencing the same tension in the workplace. The guys said, "I'm afraid to drive down the street now!"

I said, "That's how Black people feel every day." Things got better after Dr. Boxley helped us express ourselves, but they were never the same.

I learned to keep my opinions to myself. I was no longer eager to help them with their woman problems or lavish them with delicious meals. Everyone involved in the battle and fires that night received a letter of commendation from Chief Donald O. Manning. Mine says:

> *KAREN D. LASLEY-SLIDER*
> *I would like to personally extend my gratitude for your heroic efforts during the April 1992 Civil Disturbance. As I witnessed the events unfold, I thought of words such as valor, bravery, courage, and honor to describe your actions. Your valiant efforts in the face of personal danger and the most adverse conditions continued to amaze me. Firefighters and Paramedics across the nation look to you as their example of America's finest. Your performance was clearly beyond the call of duty.*

Cool words.…

———ᗡ᙭ᗡ———

After the riot (civil disturbance), I was trying to get pregnant before I was too old. I just wanted one last baby for the man of my dreams. I had already suffered two miscarriages, and I was beginning to lose hope of giving my new husband the child he wanted while he was raising my other two from Calvin. Michael told me it was okay if we didn't have another child, but I felt like I'd be short-changing him if I couldn't give him one. Some of the guys had a problem with trading shifts with me on the days I needed to go in for my doctor's visits (fertility treatments). This added to my stress, which, in turn, made it harder to get pregnant. Before my last miscarriage, the ultrasound showed I was pregnant with triplets. I was on some heavy fertility drugs. The doctor wanted me to decide on aborting one or more of the embryos if too many were growing. I told her, "I can't choose which ones will live. Either they all live, or they all die. I won't make that kind of decision."

One by one, the heartbeats of my babies disappeared. The embryonic sacks were still visible, but they were not alive. I had to get an operation to remove the dead tissue and went into a deep depression after. I slept all the time to escape the pain of my lost love ones until I had a dream that helped me.

CHAPTER 29

Dream

I was in the mall shopping with Aunt Loreen and Jewel, my Cousin Marti, Pam and my mom. Loreen came out of a store with a pair of shoes in her hand. She said, "Quick, who wears a size 10?"

Both Marti and I said, "I do!"

Loreen said, "Try them on, Kay, and see if they fit. If they don't, I'll take them back and get my money. It was such a good deal, I couldn't pass it up, and I knew one of you could fit them." I put on the shoes and walked to the other side of the mall just when an earthquake hit and split the mall in half! I was separated from my family, and I knew they were going to die!

I heard a voice in my head say, "If you stay where you are, you'll be safe, but if you try to get to them, you'll die too." I thought about all the people I would have to tell they were dead and decided it was too much to handle! I took a running start and leaped to get to them...

The next thing I remembered was floating in a tunnel, with lights and rainbows all around me. I had no physical form, but I felt sensations. I could hear other souls around me, and I could tell their age by their voices. In a blink of an eye, I was in a room teaching young souls what was right. One of the young ones was having a hard time understanding, so I decided to give an example of what was wrong so they would know the difference. Then GOD's voice told me, "No, don't teach them that, only teach them what is right. They will learn the difference on their own." Next, I remember being on a roller coaster at a high rate of speed, dipping and spinning!!! This was all sensation, without any form. Everyone I heard around me was happy and laughing. Then I heard an old soul say, "I'm bored. We do the same thing every day."

And I said, "Then why don't you be born again?"

I awoke, relieved, although I didn't believe in being born again. My religious training did not include this form of teaching. I only knew I was not depressed anymore. I felt like my babies just decided not to be born, and I knew they were not lost to me forever. I felt like I had a new understanding of why children are drawn to me. They love my spirit. I felt like GOD was telling me not to worry. Wake up and be happy; you have grieved long enough. Everything is going to be okay.

Fire Station 99 was turned into a paramedic engine company and all the firefighters were transferred to other fire stations. My next engine company assignment was Fire Station 8 (Porter Ranch area of L.A.).

Thanks for teaching me to love even when we disagree.

CHAPTER 30

Fire Station 8

This was another slow station with maybe three runs a day. I had a very cool captain who was old school, a good cook and great story-teller and jokester. He gave the impression of a Southern country gentleman with a touch of redneck. He was not a redneck by any means, but if you didn't know him, you might just think he was one at first glance. We had a good crew, and he made a deal with us. If we took care of the front office and the complaining public, he would do all the cooking. I answered the phones and did the fire prevention paperwork. Our captain had a short fuse when it came to hardheaded people with unfounded complaints.

One day, our captain had worked overtime on the shift before, and as we arrived to work, he slept in. Department policy was if we were unable to come to work for any reason, we were supposed to call in at 0630. It was around 0830 when I decided to play a trick on our captain. This was the day of the Million Man March, and all the Black people who were not marching in Washington were encouraged to stay home from work in silent protest. I called the station from the grapevine (firefighters' telephone for personal use) and pretended to be at home, saying, "Hello, Captain, this is Karen. I'm not coming into work today."

He said, "Oh, Karen, it's after 8:00. I don't know what I can do for you to keep you from being AWOL" (absent without leave).

I said, "DO WHATEVER YOU HAVE TO DO, BECAUSE I'M GOING TO SUPPORT MY PEOPLE IN THE MILLION MAN MARCH!"

He said, "YOU'RE GONNA WHAT?!!"

I said, "I'm kidding. I'm in the kitchen." (Laughing)

He came into the kitchen with his sleep hair and his hands outstretched to my neck saying, "I am going to kill you!" I got him good! He had a good sense of humor. Fire Station 8 was the place where I studied for the captain's exam and passed. Our captain made sure we had all the time and resources we needed to study. I had all kinds of ranking members coming to the station to give me mock interviews, ranging from captains to chief officers.

It was impressive, all the people who wanted to help me promote. It seemed I was always breaking tradition. The rules stated after four years of serving as a firefighter, you could promote to engineer, apparatus operator or CAPTAIN. It was the tradition for firefighters to go for the captain's position after promoting to one of the lower ranks first—engineer, apparatus operator or fire inspector. It was how the promotional ladder was climbed. But when I read that I could go directly from firefighter to captain, I decided to go for it. I did try to become an inspector first, when I was at Fire Station 99. I passed the test, but a hiring freeze caused me to die on the list.

LORREEN, RAMONA & LINDA

AARON MY ELDEST SON AND HIS WIFE DANIELLE

LILETTE, ALBERT, PAMALA & KAREN

MY HORSE PHOTO 5 YEARS OLD

JANIE BELL "MAMA" JACKSON

JANIE BELL "MAMA" JACKSON

COOTIE, JANIE BELL, DINA

RAMONA MY MOTHER

MY BROTHER ALBERT AND HIS WIFE PAM

EDEN, BLAKE, CHASE MY GRANDKIDS

BRANDON MY SECOND SON

MY GRANDMOTHER SUE "COOTIE"ARMSTEAD

MY THIRD SON DALLAS

AUNT DINA AND UNCLE CLYDE

MY SISTER LILETTE "LETTY"

LINDA MY SISTER AND HER HUSBAND DEWAYNE

RAMONA "MY MOM" UNCLE CLOUSZELL AUNT LOOEEN AND MY GRANDMOTHER "COOTIE"

MY BFF MARCIA

MY HUSBAND MICHAEL

MY SISTER PAMALA

PAMALA MY SISTER

Firefighter III Karen Lasley-Slider
Los Angeles City Fire Department
Fire Station 8, "A" Platoon

In recognition of your loyalty, superior performance,
professionalism, courage and dedication to the
Los Angeles Fire Department and the City of Los Angeles.

HAL BERNSON
Councilman, 12th District

October 19, 1995

County of Los Angeles

COMMENDATION

Karen Lasley-Slider

FIREFIGHTER III
LOS ANGELES CITY FIRE DEPARTMENT

In recognition of dedicated service
to the affairs of the community and for the
civic pride demonstrated by numerous
contributions for the benefit of all the
citizens of Los Angeles County.

OCTOBER 19, 1995

ZEV YAROSLAVSKY
Supervisor, Third District

MICHAEL D. ANTONOVICH
Supervisor, Fifth District

ME AND MY CREW

Los Angeles Fire Department
Certificate of Retirement

On behalf of the City of Los Angeles, the Los Angeles Fire Department extends its sincere thanks and appreciation to

Karen Lasley-Slider
Firefighter III

for faithfully serving 25 years with courage and loyalty, and, for providing your professional expertise and knowledge to benefit the citizens of the CITY OF LOS ANGELES in spite of personal sacrifices, obstacles and dangers. The Department offers its best wishes for a healthy, happy, and rewarding retirement.

Effective this 18th of October, 2012

Brian L. Cummings, Fire Chief

Fire Department

FIREFIGHTER

KAREN D. LASLEY-SLIDER

I would like to personally extend my gratitude for your heroic efforts during the April, 1992, Civil Disturbance.

As I witnessed the events unfold, I thought of words such as valor, bravery, courage, and honor to describe your actions.

Your valiant efforts in the face of personal danger and the most adverse conditions continued to amaze me. Firefighters and Paramedics across the nation look to you as their example of America's finest. Your performance was clearly beyond the call of duty.

DONALD O. MANNING
Chief Engineer and General Manager

MINIMUM REQUIREMENTS

AGE: At least 18 years of age, but not yet 31 years of age at the time of your nterview

EDUCATION: High School graduation or G.E.D. equivalent.

PHYSICAL: Weight (body fat content) proportionate to height.

VISION: Uncorrected distance visual acuity of at least 20/100 in the poorer eye and 20/40 in the better eye, correctable to at least 20/40 in one eye and 20/20 in the other is required. Use of contact lenses is **not** acceptable in meeting these requirements.

RESIDENCY: Applicants must become bona fide City of Los Angeles residents at the time of their Civil Service nterview and maintain such residency until completion of their probationary period. Prior to being scheduled for the Firefighter nterview you will be required to present proof of Los Angeles City residency before further processing. nterested women, who are not City residents, may submit a Firefighter notificaton card and begin participating in the special female programs, but must become bona fide City residents before their nterview will be scheduled.

Selection Process

The testing process includes a written test, which may be waived if you meet specified waiver requirements: a physical abilities test; an interview a medical including a cardiac stress test; and a background investigation. We will send you a complete explanation of the Firefighter selection process after you file a Notification Card.

CHAPTER 31

The Stentorians

Throughout my career, I have been active in recruitment for the retention of women and served on several committees with both Chief Manning and Chief Bamattre. Chief Manning was just going through the motions, following the Board of Fire Commissioners' orders and the consent decree. All of us women on the committee made several recommendations. We had concerns about childcare and recommended the possibility of splitting our shifts. It was a problem with all the single parents on the job, both male and female. But the only thing the chief allowed us to change was our dress uniform. This change allowed us the option to wear skirts instead of pants if we wanted. He also allowed us to wear diamond earrings or studs, but no hoops in our ears as long as we were on special or light duty. We wanted to look like the women we were. Baby steps, I thought.

It soon became clear to me that Chief Manning was not going to make any real changes, so I quit his committee. I felt like I was just wasting my time. He was just putting on a show for the Board of Fire Commissioners.

There was a scandal involving the women recruits in the drill tower. Someone videotaped them, showing the exhausted women barely able to perform their duties to prove women were not capable…but I knew the truth. I knew all those women on the videotape had been pushed beyond their endurance. What we saw on tape were recruits who were drilled to the breaking point! A few of the women decided to file lawsuits, claiming discrimination and harassment. This led to a City Council meeting being held with the Fire Commission investigating the reason for the videotape.

I started receiving calls from The Stentorians (an association of African American firefighters of the City of Los Angeles Fire Department, formed in 1954 to fight discrimination). They asked me to tell the story of my treatment in the drill tower. On the day of the City Council meeting, I was met by one of the firefighters before I could reach the door of the meeting. He was one who had treated me badly at Westlake. Yes, that very same one whose job I was offered. He met me in the hallway, asking if I remembered everything that happened at Westlake.

I replied, "Yes, I remember everything!"

He looked at me with pleading eyes and said, "So do I." He was afraid I was going to give his name to the City Council while telling my story. Even though the Council asked me several times who the men were who harassed me, I didn't name names. Names were not important. The truth was!

After I finished telling my story of all the obstacles I faced, of the discrimination, harassment, prejudice, I was asked by Gloria Allred what could be done to change the minds of the men concerning women doing the job of firefighters. I told her those men who already had their minds made up would not change. It was going to take new blood and time. I talked about the guys I went through the drill tower with, who had confidence in my abilities. I told her all those old firefighters who didn't believe women should be on the job would soon retire. It was the firefighters who train in the Drill Tower Academy with women who will be the change we need.

CHAPTER 32

Chief Bamattre

After the City Council meeting, Chief Manning was asked to step down. Chief Bamattre was appointed in his place. Chief Bamattre was my favorite. I felt he was sincerely interested in the retention of women when I was in Westlake's pre-training program before I became a firefighter. Chief Bamattre taught me how to change a flat tire. We were driving on the freeway to the Valley when our tire blew. He showed me step by step how to change it. Growing up, I never had to do anything like that. That was considered men's work! When he became the chief engineer, I had a direct line to his office. If I had a problem that was not being handled by my battalion chief or captain, he told me I could call him. Although I never had to, he always knew if I was having a problem with someone. He would call me before I felt the need to call him.

He was working behind the scenes. Whatever the problem was, somehow it quietly went away. He truly had my back. I love him and his beautiful wife. One of my captains was studying to be a battalion chief, and I asked him if he wanted the chief engineer to come to lunch and brainstorm with him. I knew Chief Bamattre would come if I cooked and invited him to lunch. When I asked him to help, he showed up with no hesitation. My captain was amazed that the highest-ranking person in the department came to help him. This chief engineer was another one who made me feel special and protected. My mother loved him at first sight when she met him and his wife (his wife was a beauty who made him look even better). His wife, Liz, told my mother, "Karen is his favorite. She is one of the good ones. I worry about some of the female firefighters' motives, but not Karen; she's one of the good ones."

I have a special place in my heart for both of them.

Fire Station 8 was very slow. If we had three runs a shift, that was considered a busy day. When you're studying to become a captain, you need more experience, so my captain would trade with other fire stations in the busier areas of Los Angeles. After trading with one busy station and returning home to Fire Station 8, the engine company we traded with wrote a note on the blackboard saying, "How can you live with yourself!!!?"

We called the fire station when they returned home and told them, "We get paid more by the run than you do!" LOL! They were right. I needed more experience if I was to become a captain, so I transferred to Fire Station 41.

CHAPTER 33

Fire Station 41

Fire station 41 is in Hollywood's west end. Here I was, back where I started my rookie year, Battalion 5 and it was busy! Before I arrived at Fire Station 41, all my captains had been white. This is where I had my first Black captain, who rode as a Buffalo Soldier in the parades, representing our Black cowboys! This tribute also kept the memory of our Black Confederate soldiers alive. Preserving history with his everyday life. The messed-up thing about transferring to another station was I had to prove myself again. I learned early on if you give an inch, they'll take a mile. This made me determined to nip things in the bud.

I didn't suffer in silence. If someone got on my nerves, I let them know it. I treated people with respect, and I expected the same treatment from them. It soon got around on all three shifts that "Karen, don't play!" To give you an example: There was a movie out called *Boyz N the Hood*. In this movie, there was a crackhead named Felicia. One of the guys said I looked like her. He decided my nickname would be Crackhead. It started out as a joke until a few others started calling me Crackhead. Mostly they used this name when I made a mistake of some kind, but it was no longer funny to me. I let everyone know I didn't like it and asked them to stop calling me Crackhead! Everyone got the message except my engineer. One morning after a very long night, I entered the kitchen for a cup of coffee before getting in my car to head home. I was adding cream and sugar to my coffee when my engineer started in on me. "Good morning, Crackhead," he said, with a sneaky smile on his face.

He was sitting at the kitchen table when I turned, walked over to him, balled up my right fist and brought it down on the table as hard as I could! I said, "I have told you several times, don't call me that!!! Now! I don't know what it's going to take to get through to you, but whatever it takes, I'm willing to do!!!" He apologized immediately and never called me Crackhead again. At this point, I was a seasoned firefighter working with a very young crew. I felt like I was always teaching them manners.

Again, I died on the list for a captain's position... Just one more hire and it would have been me. I left Fire Station 41 after I became pregnant with my third son, Dallas. Back to special duty I went!

The Brush Clearance Unit was happy to have me back.

CHAPTER 34

David Jr & Maceo Moore

While sleeping in the dormitory with two other firefighters, I was awakened in the early morning by my captain telling me, "Karen, you have a phone call on the business phone." I walked into the kitchen and picked up the receiver. It was a phone call from St. Vincent's Hospital. The person on the other end asked me if I knew a Gina H. Gina was the mother of my baby brother David's two sons, David Jr., and Maceo Moore (Maceo was named after Cat). Gina had a substance abuse problem, which led to me having custody of her sons for a short time. My brother David picked them up from Gina one day and dropped them off with my mother and me to take care of until Gina got back on her feet.

The nurse on the other end of the phone asked, "Are you the aunt of David and Maceo Moore?"

"Yes," I said, thinking that Gina must be in trouble again and needed me to come and pick up the boys. "Is Gina okay?"

He said yes, but he was trying to contact my brother. He was sorry to tell me that my two nephews had died in a fire. It's funny how you can't believe your ears when you hear bad news for the first time. I don't know how many times he repeated the same information. I do know when I finally processed the information, I kept repeating the same thing over and over again, "What? Oh no... They died in a fire? They DIED in a FIRE?" The nurse finally brought me back to my senses. He told me I had to contact my mother and tell her.

My mother lived with Little Linda and Dwayne at the time. Linda had just given birth to twins, and our mother had moved in to help her take care of the babies until they were potty-trained. She potty-trained all of her grandchildren and took care of them while we worked. My captain must've been listening on the other extension because he came into the kitchen and took the phone from me. He gathered more information from the nurse on the line and then called our battalion chief to inform him we were out of service and needed a department chaplain. I went into the locker room and called my mother on the grapevine. My brother-in-law, Dwayne, answered the phone. I told him he had to wake up Mom and tell her... her grandsons, David and Maceo, had just died in a fire. I told Dwayne, "You have to tell her...because I can't!!!"

He woke up my sister instead and told Linda, "Kay just called and said David and Maceo just died in a fire..."

Linda said, "I know, someone just came and told me." She thought she was dreaming. (Angels...her father, Big Al.) The battalion chief showed up at Fire Station 8 after what seemed like forever...I had to sit and wait for him; they wouldn't let me drive my own car home. They were worried about me. The chief's aide drove my car with me in the passenger seat. I was numb with grief. As I walked into my house, Pam was on the phone talking to our cousin Debbie. As usual, Debbie had something negative to say. I told Pam to tell Debbie if she was going to have a negative attitude, to keep her ass at home! Our family always comes together in a crisis; we draw strength from one another. And because my mother was staying at Little Linda's house, that was where we would all be.

But first I had to go to the hospital and check on Gina. As I walked through the doors of St. Vincent's Hospital, I could smell the residue of smoke. This was further confirmation to me that I was not caught in a nightmare! The fire department chaplain met me in the lobby and showed me to Gina's room. He had arrived before me and started consoling her. When I walked into the room, she was lying in bed with her face to the wall. I asked, "Are you okay?"

She turned to me with tear-filled eyes and said, "Yes, I'm okay."

"What happened?"

134

She said, "I was renting the garage part of a house where a lot of people were staying. It was cold, so I brought a space heater. I turned it on to keep them warm and left. I was gone for only a little while…I was on my way back when I heard the sirens…I felt it in my gut! Something was wrong; those sirens were for me! I had on flip-flops, and they were holding me back, so I kicked them off, and started to run!

"When I got to the house, everyone was outside watching the firemen put out the fire. I went to them one by one and asked them, 'Where are my babies?' No one would look at me! No one would answer me! I tried to get past the firefighters to get inside to find them, but they kept pushing me back! I started screaming…and they called the ambulance and brought me here."

I could tell just by looking at her that she had left the boys alone to go get high. Her guilt was written all over her face. My heart went out to her. She had paid the ultimate price. I wrapped my arms around her and told her to tell the police she went to the store. I didn't want anyone to hurt her anymore. No jail could punish her more than the loss of her sweet, loving little boys. She was discharged to my care, and we went to be with my mother and our family at Little Linda's house.

CHAPTER 35

City of Angeles

It was a gray, rainy day, and I was happy it was raining. It seemed a sin for the sun to shine on a sad day like today. The weather reflected our mood. It took three of us, my sister-in-law Pam; Al's wife, myself and Gina, to plan the funeral. We needed Gina to sign the paperwork, me to organize where we were going and get us there and back, and Pam to talk to the people we had arranged to meet.

I could barely function, and Gina was lost! The three of us made one whole person. We could not and would not try to manage on our own. Whenever someone wanted to separate us, we would tell whoever it was, "No! We need to stick together!" We all stayed together at Linda and Dwayne's house in Carson, California. I lived in the San Fernando Valley, and all Gina's appointments were in the City of Los Angeles.

The first day we set out to make arrangements, I had a quarter tank of gas in my Toyota Previa minivan. I told Pam and Gina to remind me to stop and get gas before we ran out. We traveled from Carson to the heart of Los Angeles and then to the San Fernando Valley. When we arrived back at Linda's house, in Carson, I looked down at the gas gauge. It was still on one-quarter tank of gas. The next day, we set out to meet with the Red Cross, in Gardena, CA. They gave Gina money to move and buy clothes. From Gardena, we went to Rosewood Cemetery, in Los Angeles, to pick out a casket. Although the boys were cremated, we felt a casket would help the younger ones to understand the boys' death better. When we finished our business, I drove back to my house in the Valley to get a change of clothes before heading back to Linda's. As we got out of the car on the second day of running around and making arrangements, I looked at my gas gauge again. It was still on one-quarter of a tank of gas! I couldn't believe my eyes, so I asked Gina and Pam if I was crazy. We had been driving for two days, and the level on the gas meter never moved!

On the third day, after leaving Linda's house, we said our prayers. We thanked GOD for all his blessings and the miracle of not running out of GAS! And I promised to fill it up at the next gas station I saw. It was 3:00 p.m. when I looked down at the gas tank that was still at one-quarter tank. I told Gina and Pam to look at the gauge. We were astounded!!! I pulled into the next gas station I saw and filled up then and there. I felt GOD was looking out for us. And running out of gas would've been the last straw! He protected us from that! God gave Gina everything she asked for and things she didn't know she needed. But all she really wanted was her babies back.

Letter of Appreciation:

Dear Chief Manning, I received a call at 4:30 AM on February 16, 1994, telling me that my two little nephews were killed in a fire. This is the worst thing that ever happened to my family and me. I didn't have the slightest idea how to arrange a funeral or help my family cope with the disaster of losing not one but two of the cutest little boys you could ever hope to meet. I can truly say it was a blessing being at work when I received the news. I say this because Chief Cornwell took charge of the situation and arranged for the Department Chaplain, Captain Hilliger, to meet us at the hospital where my sister-in-law had been transported, after learning from the Lynnwood Fire Chief her only children had not survived the house fire. Captain Hilliger arrived at the hospital ahead of me. He consoled my sister-in-law and helped her to start the healing process. I believe she would have lost her mind if one more person denied her the human kindness Capt. Hilliger so freely gave. There are so many people I feel should be brought to your attention, people who were there and will always have a special place in my heart. Dr. Boxley offered his services to me in helping the children understand what happened to David and Maceo. They kept asking the same questions over and over again. "How did David and Maceo die? And how could they die, when they're kids?" After a session with Dr. Boxley, they understood. They wrote letters and added pictures to send to David and Maceo by way of balloons, on the day of the funeral. It was so beautiful, all the balloons being released at the same time and making it through the trees and going up into the blue sky. The children felt they could talk to David and Maceo whenever they wanted to. They promised to send letters and pictures regularly (I find myself releasing balloons sometimes too, just to kiss them). The members of Fire Station 99 and 8, who filled my home with flowers and living plants. I have never felt more love. Someone even sent flowers to the chapel. Thank you. The Relief Association, Captain Dolan for his sound advice on funding. He made it clear the Relief Association would loan me any funds I needed if it became necessary. Thanks to his advice, it was not. Chief Jimmy Hill, Captain Hilliger, and Dr. Boxley for sticking with me to the bitter end and representing the fire department at the funeral. They gave me the strength to do what no one else in my family could and that was to bury our babies. There are those who need training in dealing with people in the midst of tragedy. Not these people, They can

give lessons. May God reward them for the Spirit
they show. (AMEN)
    I THANK THEM ALL
                                 Karen Lasley-Slider

I couldn't wait to get back to work. Something had to be done; too many people were dying in fires. I called the Fire Prevention Bureau and asked them if they had any programs that would deal with this issue. I was told they had a school outreach program. This program taught preschoolers through fourth graders fire prevention in the hopes of saving other children from the fate of my nephews. Something good had to come out of their deaths! (Beauty for my ashes.) We taught the children how to dial 911. How and why to stop, drop and roll. To crawl out of the fire. We taught them that the closer they were to the ground, the more likely they were to find fresh air. We taught them not to hide from us when we came to fight the fire. Even if they made a mistake. We donned our breathing apparatus so they could hear the sound and know it was us, coming to rescue them. It was a joy knowing the children had tools to use, in case of a fire or emergency medical situation. We made them the teachers to their families.

    I worked in special duty until Dallas was born then I was transferred to Fire Station 91.

CHAPTER 36

Fire Station 91

This station is a single engine with a rescue located in Sylmar, in the San Fernando Valley. Dallas was four months old when I went back to work as a firefighter. It was a new experience for the guys having a lactating firefighter. My family doesn't believe in bottles for feeding, except in emergencies. We are required to breastfeed our babies for the first year of their life, if possible. But most definitely just after giving birth. I can't tell you how many times we were out hydrant testing, or on a run, or shopping for dinner when the crew had to drop everything to take me back to the fire station so I could pump my breast milk for Dallas's next-day supply. I stored it in the fire station's freezer, and the guys would come running out of the station to my car to remind me if I got into my car without it! They didn't want any confusion. SOD (scheduled overtime duty) guys might think it was homemade ice cream and taste it. LOL! It was a good and bad thing working close to home. The good was that I could drop by the house if we were near my home and check on my baby. The bad was the possibility something would happen to someone I knew, and we'd respond to the incident. Fortunately, I never had to deal with this problem.

Foothill Boulevard was known for street racing on the weekends. It wasn't uncommon for us to go to the scene of a bad traffic accident with fatalities. It was always nerve-racking responding, not knowing if we would find one of my neighbors, or worse, one of my teenage sons. After the incident, I would immediately call home and check on my kids. It never failed with these racing traffic accidents that either Aaron or Brandon knew the teenagers involved. This led to me pleading with them not to race and tell their friends not to either.

My children listen to me…. Ask Aaron about that time I told him and his friends to go home when I saw them at Grandma Cootie's apartment. They stopped by for Sunday dinner. She always cooked Sunday dinner. She knew her grandchildren showed up just for the food and or to visit her. She always made my favorite foods when I did her hair. This was one of those days. Aaron and two of his friends who lived with us in the Valley walked in… and my heart sank, I felt they were in danger. I said to them, "What are you doing in L.A.?"

Aaron said, "They needed to get some clothes and we are hungry. I told them I know my Grandma Cootie cooked, so we came to eat."

I said, "Here is some money. Go home, go straight home. Do not stop and buy any food in L.A.! Go home to the Valley. Now, go straight home." They were curious, but they obeyed and headed home.

When they arrived in the Valley, they decided to stop at a IN and Out Burger stand. It was there that Aaron recalled my words as a gangbanger (not Black) pulled a gun on him for turning his back and walking away; after he was asked what set he was from. Aaron said as he felt the gun pointed at his head, the thought went through my mind, *My mother told me to go straight home.*

This is why we pray every day. God is Amazing. HE protects HIS Own.

CHAPTER 37

Las Vegas

My mother, Ramona, loved Las Vegas! September 7, 1941, is her birthday, and she required a trip to Las Vegas every year. She was a diabetic and heavy smoker (weed and cigarettes). Her medical condition meant we had to get a room with a kitchen, so she could store food to eat regularly, and the smoking meant she needed a balcony. One year, Pamala, our cousin Marti (Marriyan Hill), my husband, Michael, and I went with her to Vegas. We had a two-bedroom suite, with Pam and Mom in one room, Michael and I in the other and Marty on the fold out sofa-couch. My mother wasn't feeling well this trip, so we left her in the room while we gambled. She didn't complain, but she didn't eat much either.

On our last night in Las Vegas, Pam woke us, knocking on our bedroom door, saying, "Something's wrong with Mom!" My mother was lying in bed sweating profusely, burping and passing gas.

She was alert and oriented when I asked, "What's wrong?"

She said, "I just feel heavy."

"Heavy?" I asked her. "What does that mean?"

She couldn't explain it any other way and kept saying, "I just feel heavy." I thought about all the times I'd been on calls with the paramedics at Fire Station 91. Whenever they couldn't get a clear understanding of why we were called, the one question they would always ask the patient was, "Have you ever felt this way before?"

When the patient said, "No," they got a ride to the hospital. I reached back to that training and asked my mother, "Have you ever felt this way before?"

She said, "No, never!" Michael immediately got on the phone and called 911. He even went outside and waited for the paramedics to arrive so he could show them to our room. Two firefighters, EMTs, arrived ahead of the paramedic rescue. They were the same rank as me, and from their questions I could tell they were trying to blow Mom's symptoms off. They thought she had food poisoning. While they were taking her vital signs, she kept burping and passing gas. One of the EMTs said several times, "Wow, she has a lot of gas!"

Finally, I told him, "Yes!! She has a lot of gas! Now, I don't know what's going on...but something's wrong! Because she never complains!" When the paramedic rescue arrived, they hooked her up to the cardiac monitor. By now she was complaining of left shoulder pain also. The monitor showed a tombstone EKG rhythm. A HEART ATTACK!

Diabetics are known for having silent heart attacks. Pam had gathered Mom's purse, medications, and coat. I thought she wanted to ride to the hospital with Mom as I watched her with her arms full of our mother's belongings. When I asked her if she was going with Mom, she shoved all those things into my arms as if to say No, stupid! In the back of the rescue ambulance, my mother never stopped answering the female paramedic's questions on the way to the emergency room. You know, the basics... "What's your name; what day is it; who's the President; what kind of medication do you take?" On the way to the hospital, just as happens in Los Angeles, we were diverted to another hospital due to emergency room saturation. Now Michael, Pam, and Marti were on their way to the wrong hospital. I called them and gave them the new information.

ST. ROSE HOSPITAL

While they were transferring my mother from the gurney to the emergency room bed, she went into ventricular fibrillation (v-fib).

Her eyes rolled back, and she started to have convulsions. She caught the emergency staff off guard! While the paramedic, doctor, and nurses ran for the crash cart, to revive her, I lowered my mother's head so her body would be in the flat position when they shocked her heart into a normal rhythm. All the while I was stroking her hair and telling her everything was going to be okay. It seemed like it took forever for them to get it together.

They were back at her bedside. The paramedic had the paddles in her hands and charged for shocking, but they were still looking for the pads to stick to her chest. My mother had been convulsing for too long in my opinion. I said, "DO something! Do something now!"

That's when the doctor who was still looking in the crash cart for the pads said, "Shock her now! Just go ahead and shock her!" The first shock didn't work; the second one did. I stood at the foot of her bed when one of the nurses was trying to shoo me out. I crossed my arms in front of my chest and told him I wasn't going anywhere! I told him I knew what was going on. I knew how bad it was, but I was not going anywhere! The paramedic who transported her to the hospital told the nurse I was okay because I was also a firefighter. When they started taking Mom's blood pressure and the rest of her vital signs, I went outside of the emergency room to call my husband.

He answered the phone on the first ring, and I said, "Mom just coded in the emergency room."

"You ARE shitting me!" was all he said.

I asked him, "Are Marti and Pam sitting there listening to you?"

It seemed to me, by the pause on the phone, that Michael was looking around in the car for them before he told me, "No. I dropped them off at the emergency room entrance while I parked the car." I went back in the emergency room to see how my mother was doing. Thinking the absolute worst! All the while, a tiny voice in my head kept reassuring me. I thought… this is bad…this is really bad! Of all the runs I've been on in my career, those people who had problems like Mom, died. That's when that tiny voice in my head told me, "This is where the success rates are…people that code in the hospital are in the right place when they code." I kept thinking if she would just open her eyes and look at me, I'd know she'd be okay.

I repeated this over and over in my head, "Open your eyes, Mom, and look at me... Open your eyes. Open your eyes!" And she did. She opened her eyes with a look on her face that said, "Why are you bugging me to open my eyes; can't you see I'm tired?" I was so relieved.... Again, I stroked her hair, told her everything was going to be okay and to close her eyes and get some sleep. She drifted back to sleep, an easy sleep, a healing sleep.

I looked up to see Pam at the foot of Mom's bed with a panicked look on her face as she watched the chaos of the doctors and nurses around her. I motioned for her to follow me out of the area. I told her Mom was in bad shape. Pam started to fall apart as we walked to the waiting-room. I explained to her what happened on our way to the hospital. How she coded when she was transferred from the gurney to the hospital bed. I gave her a rushed account. I had to get back to Mom! I told her she had to pull herself together before she came back to sit with Mom because she couldn't let Mom see her like that! I held her in my arms as she cried. We were in the room they put you in when they don't expect the person in the hospital to survive. I told Pam to get it all out because I was going to need her later when I fell apart.

And she did get it all out... and was there when I needed her.

On my way back to sit at my mother's bedside, I saw the male nurse who had tried to shoo me away when Mom came in. He had a pitying look on his face like my mother was already dead. I returned his pity with a fierce look of my own that said, "Don't look at me like that! My mother is not dead!" When I got to my mother's bedside, the emergency room doctor told me Mom had coded again!

All I could say was, "Oh no, oh no!" before I heard the doctor say, "But!! We got her back! Do you hear me? We got her back!"

I decided then and there I was never leaving her alone as long as she was hospitalized because she would never leave me. From then on, Pam was posted on one side at the foot of Mom's bed and I was on the other. I felt like we were avenging angels guarding her, and nothing bad could happen as long as one of us was with her.

Eventually, as everyone else arrived, all six of us (her children) were taking turns sleeping at her bedside. That was until Lilette showed up and refused to move out of the bedside spot and give us a turn. It's a good thing she needed to take a shower, or she would have never given us a chance back at Mom's bedside. She needed a break but was too stubborn to admit it. I was exhausted, too tired to argue, and I was glad she was with us. The love of our family would keep Mom safe. GOD LOVES US! He loves the faith we have in him. We know from experience nothing is impossible for our Father in Heaven. WE ARE A PRAYING FAMILY!

As soon as he could, Michael called everyone—my grandmother, my aunts, my siblings—and they called others. The emergency room phone was ringing off the hook. The hospital staff kept telling the doctor, "Another one's on the phone!" They had never experienced this kind of love for one person. Everywhere we followed Mom inside the hospital, for x-rays and tests, the doctors and nurses told people how loving our family was. Complete strangers were saying to us, "Oh, you're that family everyone is talking about." Pure love! The next day, the hospital waiting room was filled with our family. We all took turns sitting by her bedside. We changed shifts, like the hospital changed shifts. She was never alone. Pam and I gave her, her bath every day and changed her sheets. The nurses loved having Mom as a patient because all they had to do was give her medicine.

My family has a medical background. We came from midwives (The Sangoma's are African Healers, Natural healers) and nurses. We know how hectic working in a hospital can be, and at the same time we know that the patients who have family members checking on them receive the best care. No one could take better care of her than we did. She needed a stent in her heart to keep her artery open. Her heart had a 90 percent blockage. Time was of the essence! I felt so guilty! Here I was a firefighter for one of the best fire departments in the world, one that offered us a free education to become paramedics, and I had not taken advantage of it! I knew if my mother died, I would never forgive myself! So...I made it my goal to become a paramedic as soon as this crisis was over. God willing.

It was a good thing Mom won money in Las Vegas before she got sick because everyone else spent theirs. We used her winnings to stay longer in our hotel while we took care of her. Everyone who came to Las Vegas to be with Mom ended up staying at the same hotel with us. It was a blessing! We were all together, room hopping. Keeping each other strong. And Mona (Ramona Jane Cunningham) pulled through like a champ! God loves us. Prayer works!

FAITH THE SIZE OF A MUSTARD SEED CAN MOVE MOUNTAINS!!!

PARAMEDIC SCHOOL

I had sixteen years on the department as a firefighter and more years experience in the medical field, from working at Kaiser as a CNA/Orderly. The idea of paramedic school did challenge me...I had been out of school for a long time, and studying didn't come easy for me. Math had always been my weakness. I was educated in the Los Angeles Unified School District. This was not the best education, in my humble opinion. I knew others who read books required for graduation...not so in my neighborhood. There were only two sworn members in my paramedic class. An engineer who also wished to promote and me. The rest of the class was made up of explorers with young, eager minds that absorbed everything like sponges.

They had a formula for New Math that made absolutely no sense to me. I made the instructors break the metric system down into dollars and cents, so a baby could understand it! I was worried I would make a mistake and give the wrong amount of drugs to my patients. Not on my watch! My baby, Dallas, was a toddler at the time and couldn't understand why his mother was always studying when she was at home. The study load was huge! Our instructors told us, "You are going to eat an elephant, one bite at a time." And we did. I read the chapters in the books, highlighted them, made flash cards and tapes to listen to whenever I was traveling in the car.

We were given quizzes daily in preparation for our block exams. We had to maintain an 85 percent average. If we failed one block exam, we were out of the paramedic program. The first time we had a block exam, I stopped the instructor before we started the test and asked, "Can I say a prayer before we get started?" I knew how badly we all wanted to be successful; I was calling for all the help we could get! I didn't care what they thought of me as I prayed out loud for all of us to pass. I was pleased no one objected. After that first time, I was called to pray before every block exam. They felt the power of prayer!

On the day of our final exam to receive our paramedic license, we had an outside instructor who didn't know about our habit of praying before exams. On the previous occasions, I would just start praying. This time I was just going to pray silently. One of the students stopped the instructor before he called time for the exam and told him, "Wait, Karen has to pray first!" This was one of my proudest moments as a Christian! We lost a few along the way, but the majority of the students passed paramedic school.

And I know God found a few more of his people to call on Him in prayer...John 3:16-21.

16

For God so loved the world, that he gave his only begotten Son, that whosoever believeth in him should not perish, but have everlasting life.

17

For God sent not his Son into the world to condemn the world; but that the world through him might be saved.

18

He that believeth in him is not condemned: but he that believeth not is condemned already, because he hath not believed in the name of the only begotten Son of God.

19

And this is the condemnation, that light is come into the world, and men loved darkness rather than light, because their deeds were evil.

20

For everyone that doeth evil hateth the light, neither cometh to the light, lest his deeds should be reproved.

21

But he that doeth truth cometh to the light, that his deeds may be made manifest, that they are wrought in God. (Excerpt from *The Holy Bible - King James Version.*)

CHAPTER 38

Fire Station #57

My first assignment as a dual function firefighter/paramedic was in South Central Los Angeles. I grew up in this area, but it no longer resembled the place of my childhood memories! We used to walk everywhere we went. We walked from my grandmother's apartment, on 39th Street between Vermont and Budlong, to my apartment on 82nd Street, between Hoover and Vermont. At the age of twelve and thirteen years old. We didn't have a care in the world.

As I looked around the neighborhood in my new assignment, gangs, drugs, and hopelessness was the majority of what I saw! The people who lived here used 911 like it was their personal taxi service. Pregnant women made no plans to get to the hospital on their own, even with nine months to get ready for the event. Their plan was to call 911. Some of these people would have two cars parked in their driveway and call 911 for transportation! Why? I would ask. They thought if they went by ambulance they would be seen faster. I let my disappointment be known! Every time I came in contact with this problem of 911 abuse, I let them know how wrong they were. I told them about the people who received delayed care because of their selfishness. I let them know who they were hurting the most.

People were getting shot, hurt in car accidents and dying because of their selfishness. I told them the next time they called without a real emergency, I was not going to be happy! One night it was raining cats and dogs. At 3:00 in the morning, we got a call from a frequent 911 abuser. The engine co. started complaining and warning us, the paramedics, to be careful because this patient had psych problems and was known to get physical. This patient lived upstairs in the back house. He was still in bed when we arrived. I asked, "Why did you call 911?"

He told me, "In my home, I am the king of this castle!"

I told him, "I am the queen of that rescue ambulance, and if you don't get dressed fast, we are leaving you!"

He got dressed (laughing) and we carried him down the stairs and put him in the rescue for transport. That's when he started getting belligerent! I was driving, and my white male partner was in the back with him taking his vital signs. He threatened to beat up my partner because he didn't like the way he looked at him. I stopped the rescue, pulled over, and switched places with my partner. I told my patient, "You can't beat up my partner because I need him to work with me for the rest of the shift." And he calmed down.

This is an example of the type of runs we went on, on a daily basis. Poor people, mentally ill people, and those who thought we were here just to serve them! This attitude seemed to be the norm in both the rich and poor areas of Los Angeles. The 911 abuse was so prevalent we had to go out of service just to restock the rescue with life-saving supplies. Bogus calls, on top of shootings, stabbings, traffic accidents and really sick people on a daily basis wore us out! All I could do was sleep when I got home from a hard night's work. Many days we went without food and sleep due to the call load. Add to this young, white males who come from very different backgrounds and the prejudice echoes just came out. I felt like I was waging war on both sides—for and against both the public and the department. For example...

It was the middle of the night, around Christmas. We got a call for an unknown medical problem. The EMTs on the 800 series arrived a few minutes before the paramedic rescue. When we (the paramedics) pulled up, my partner said to me, "Stay in the rig, Karen; I'll l handle it." I watched my partner and the EMTs through the window and warmth of the rescue, on a cold night, as they talked to a man sitting in a chair in his front yard. It looked like they were trying to persuade the man to go to the hospital. Standing next to the man were two concerned ladies. They looked like they were getting angry with my crew. I got out of the rig to find out what was wrong.

As I approached, I could see this man was in distress. He was short of breath; he had on a security guard uniform, but his pants were wet. His legs were swollen from calf to thigh. His skin was weeping fluid through his pants. It was plain to see his body was doing everything it could to keep him alive. I asked him why he didn't want to go to the hospital. He said, "I need to work to buy Christmas gifts for my kids." I told him he was going to ruin Christmas for his kids if he died for toys! He had been sick for a long time, and his body was using its backup system to keep him

I told him, "You need to go with us now!" I refused to take NO for an answer! The ladies that were with him were irate. They told me that the other firefighters were refusing to take him. They said, "This has been going on a long time."

"And what made you call tonight?"

The ladies expressed to me they had been trying to get their friend to go to the hospital for a long time. They were the ones that called, not him. They felt like the other firefighters didn't care and were trying to brush them, and him, off. They thought it was a Black vs. White thing!

I dismissed the EMTs and told my partner to get the gurney. We were transporting this patient to the hospital. After transferring the patient to the hospital, on our way back to the fire station, I asked my partner, "Why didn't you want to take that man to the hospital?"

He said, "We are not a taxi service! He's been sick a long time. What made him pick tonight to go to the hospital?"

I said, "We are exactly that! A taxi service. From now on, anyone who wants a ride to the hospital is getting one, especially the sick ones. I worked hard for this paramedic license, and I'm not going to lose it because you don't want to transport someone to the hospital!"

I soon left Fire Station 57 because I couldn't deal with the attitudes. It got so bad I thought someone slashed my tires on my car. Turns out it was a defect in the tires that made them look like they had been slashed. There was a BIG INVESTIGATION!

I transferred back to fire Station 82 in Hollywood as a dual function firefighter/paramedic, assigned to the Rescue Ambulance.

MY OLD ROOKIE HOUSE, FIRE STATION 82

Fire Station 82 is another busy house to work in, never a dull moment. I loved it! I loved my captain and I loved my crew. I loved the excitement of the district. Hollywood had it all. Brushfires, high-rise fires, physical rescues, hazardous materials incidents and movie stars needing something. This district was full of up-and-coming firefighters ready to promote. Be it to apparatus operator, engineer, inspector, or captain. Those who were Captain 1 and Captain ll were on their way to promoting to battalion chief. It was exciting and challenging work.

The problem with working in Hollywood was everyone was on his or her way someplace else. I went through three captains at Fire Station 82. The last captain I worked for was a hard man. He was young, had less time on the job than I, and was a micromanager. With seniority comes certain privileges....I had more seniority than anyone on my shift, probably on all three shifts, and my captain wanted to assign to me a Boot's job. A Boot is someone who has less time than everyone else in the fire station but is off probation. A Boot gets all the undesirable jobs. Fire prevention coordinator is one. I had already served my time when I worked at Fire Station 8, but my new captain decided that this was to be my added duty.

We were eating lunch at the kitchen table when he announced, "We need a new fire prevention coordinator, and Karen, I want you to be it!"

I looked at him and said, "That's a Boot's job, and I don't feel like running calls all day on the rescue, with the added responsibility of scheduling fire prevention inspections. No, thank you."

He said, "Karen, this may reflect on your evaluation."

I said, "Are you going to recommend me for termination? No? Then I don't care how it reflects my evaluation."

He gave me a DIRECT ORDER to be the FPC. A direct order is a command that is not used lightly. It was unfair! I replied, "Okay, I'm outta here." I started putting in my transfer request that same day. Every shift, he had three or four Brownies on his desk to sign. He got tired of signing them and permitted me to sign his name in his place.

I put in for a nice quiet place in Brentwood, Fire Station 19. This was an assignment that needed high seniority. I was close to retirement; my plan was twenty years. I had eighteen years on the job at this time, and it was not enough? Or so my captain thought. He had a comment every shift, trying to persuade me to stay under his command. I got the transfer to Fire Station 19 and was ready to settle down to wait out my time till retirement. My back, shoulders, neck, and knees hurt constantly. It was time to take it easy. In a slow station, I could buy some time. My plan was so close; I could see the light at the end of the tunnel...

CHAPTER 39

Fire Station 19

Brentwood, California, rich people, and good medical care; it's amazing what money can do in your life. You eat only the freshest of food, organic this and that. Farmers Markets and Whole Foods were the places to shop in Brentwood. The best doctors and private nurses money can buy will allow you to live a long and productive life.

I thought about all those poor people who live in the war-torn parts of Los Angeles. I thought about how unfair it was. They were dying like flies in South Central Los Angeles. They, who rely on the County hospitals. The rich people don't have a clue about how unbalanced medical care is. The rich are always talking about the handouts but are not willing to give a hand up. I thought about the Republicans surrounding me when Obama was running for the forty forth Presidency. I was on duty election night. I was so excited for this new era, the possibilities of it all, a *Black President!* All my co-workers were Republicans and refused to watch the news reports as the results were coming in. It looked like the Democrats were winning, and I was glued to the T.V. chair. I called everyone I knew to celebrate how close we were. No one I talked to wanted to get his or her hopes up. Finally!!! My friend Marsha was willing to see the outcome I did. We were going to WIN! I lived to not only see the first Black President of the United States of America; I voted for him! Even my Grandma Cootie lived long enough to cast her VOTE!

I went into the dorm room and fell asleep with a smile on my face. I was the only happy voter in the Fire Station, this historic day in Black history! Early the next morning we were awakened from our sleep for an altered-level-of-consciousness call. Our patient was a diabetic whose blood sugar level had dropped too low. He was snoring in a coma-like sleep as I established a line and pushed the D-50 to wake him. He was a wealthy Jewish man who lived in a large and beautiful estate.

As he opened his eyes and looked at me, the first thing he said to me when he became alert was, "YOU MUST BE SO HAPPY!"

I said, "Well, yes, I am. I'm glad you're okay."

He said, "No! Not about me. About Obama! I voted for him. We raised a lot of money for his campaign. We are so glad he won!"

I said, "I am!!! I had no one to celebrate with all day until you! All my co-workers are Republicans. I'm so glad I got this call and came here to wake you up! Now I can celebrate." The guys went back to the rig while I stayed inside to talk with my newfound friend. I had to go to a stranger's house to celebrate the first Black President.... Not all rich people are oblivious to the needs of the common people.

—⁂—

While working at Fire Station 19, I had a great partner named George. George was a Macho man and not easy on those who are weak. We worked well together on all our calls. On a cardiac arrest, the rescue and the engine company work in perfect harmony. This is what happens when you work with the same people over and over again; you learn what needs to be done, and you just fall in place. At this stage of my career, I was starting to feel my back pain. All those years as a firefighter have taken their toll on my body. Although I'm trained as a firefighter and paramedic, whenever we respond to the fire calls, the guys are demanding less and less of me. They watched me as I performed my duties around the station and knew if I was having a good or bad day just by my posture. On the bad days, they made sure I didn't carry anyone up or downstairs; they do all the heavy lifting, squatting and pulling. On the days when they couldn't avoid having me do my share, the days I was forced to pull my weight, not long after the incident was over, my pain would cause me to go off-duty.

I stayed off-duty longer, due to my long history of injury and age; I didn't heal as fast as I used to. Bad shoulders, knees, and spine, the curse of the job. But my back problem is the worst of them. I felt guilty about not pulling my weight, but the guys assured me I make up for it by cooking for them. I hated being on special duty, doing secretarial work. You never knew where you are going to end up while you are healing. They could put you someplace close to your home or far away. I had been on special duty so often, I just called around to some of my old spots to see if they needed me again. I usually found a place to go on my own. It was a cool feeling knowing they wanted me to come back. One of the things that sucks is working four days a week, ten hours a day. My normal shift as a firefighter paramedic was three days a week, twenty-four hours a day, alternating every other day and off-duty four days. My family loved the schedule; it makes for some interesting staycations. We love to beat the crowds. Imagine going to a theme park on a weekday, no lines or short ones. We plan vacations any time of the year; no need to wait for summertime. Our kids learned to ski and snowboard and have gone on cruises around the world. They have the life I could have never even dreamed about as a child. When I tell them stories of my childhood, they think I'm exaggerating.

Our whole family is very close. We crave each other's company. We are always happy to get together and love on each other. People we meet are drawn to us because of this. And with the little ones coming up, we continue to grow in size. One of the things our mother taught us was: We are wealthy as long as we have each other. I know I will never be homeless as long as my brothers or sisters have a place to live. I will never be hungry as long as my brothers and sisters have food to eat. I will never be in financial need as long as one of my brothers or sisters can lend or give me money.

There was a movie called *Soul Food*. It focused on a family with a strong matriarch, who cooked Sunday dinner after church. My sister Pamala decided our family was getting too large and the little cousins didn't know each other, so we needed to start getting together more often. Pam came up with our own Soul Food Sunday. It was once a month, with everyone alternating hosting. The whole family was invited. Pam had a two-bedroom apartment and asked if her day to Host Soul Food Sunday could be at my house; my house is a two-story single family made for gatherings. The front and back yard have an open feel and a place for children and adults. It was the way to bring our family closer together. And show up we all did, from Great-Grandma Cootie to second and third cousins with kids playing upstairs, downstairs and outside. Noise everywhere. Grandma Cootie would sit in Michael's recliner with a smile on her face. I asked her what she was smiling about. She said, "My house used to sound like this all the time." She loved the noise.

CHAPTER 40

Pamala Sue Lark

Pamala Sue Lark was born May 4, 1957. She was the person the younger ones asked for advice because she was a free spirit who lived life. If you told her a secret, you never knew if she would keep it to herself or spread it to the world. She was always poking her nose in everyone else's business. If I thought she told any of my secrets; I would say to her all the time, "Pam, you can't hold water!"

She said, "Kay, you think I tell everything, but I don't! When I'm gone, you will see, I didn't tell everything!" My sister was always trying to make ends meet, and she was not above cleaning your house to make extra money. Her kids had the best of everything. They wore the latest fashions and always had the new sneakers that came out, no matter the cost. She would make it happen if it was her desire. She lost Shonnie's father to drugs early in life. She was just sixteen years old when Gregory Taylor died of a heroin overdose. Shonnie was a baby and never knew her handsome father. Pam and I were always together as children and not much changed when we became adults. We supported each other through heartache and poverty. As youngsters, we fought each other and anyone else who hurt those we loved.

Pam's son, Kraig, was her second born. His father was abusive. His name was also Kraig. I never understood why she kept going back to him and taking his shit! She was the perfect housewife. She cooked and cleaned and was proud of her lovemaking skills. She would shock you with her outbursts on a regular basis. She didn't care where we were. In public around strangers was her favorite place to make you blush. The more people she could shock the better. She was the kind of person who would flash her naked body at you right after a bath or shower. I loved her with the love and respect of a reserved younger sister who wished she was as free spirited. She was considerate of others, always thinking of ways to make you happy.

After another family member's funeral, she asked me to play hooky from work the next day. We'd had so many deaths in our family lately, we were becoming numb to the pain. She wanted me to spend the night with her. But I needed to go to work. I said, "On my four days off we can hang out." We had just brought in the new year with a fun party on the eve of 2007. This was going to be the year Pam kicked her no-good man to the curb! She wrote down all the reasons why he needed to go.

Pam wrote:

THINGS I DON'T LIKE

1. Not knowing where you are.
2. Not answering my page until you're ready.
3. Forgetting about me.
4. Fucking around on me and having a baby.
5. Don't spend enough time with me.
6. When you take me to the store and sit in the car.
7. Talking on the phone, wanting me to be quiet.
8. Saying you'll pay a bill and never do.
9. Come home, hurry to make love and then leave.
10. Don't caress me enough.
11. We don't have any fun together.
12. I haven't met your mom.
13. Almost six years into this relationship, you haven't committed to me.
14. Asking you to do something and you make excuses.
15. You never ask me if I need anything.

THINGS I REQUIRE FROM YOU

1. Be at my family gatherings.
2. Be my best friend.
3. Think about me even when you're away from me and how much I love you.
4. Always be true.
5. Get my bracelet, ten months late to date.
6. Spend a lot of your time home with me.
7. When I page you, answer in a timely manner.
8. Help me get a new car.
9. Help you get a new truck.
10. Get a home.
11. To have a strong Love no one can break.
12. Bring your Horny Ass home to me.

I'm here to give you what you want! Freak me, Daddy!

CHAPTER 41

Daisy's Call

While I was driving to the hospital to drop off a patient, my cell phone rang. It's unprofessional to answer your phone while treating a patient, so I waited until I finished with my patient and was outside the hospital to check my caller I.D. As I looked at the phone, I saw it was Daisy, my great-niece, Pam's granddaughter. My first thought was, Daisy never calls; she must be having trouble cashing the check I gave her for getting good grades in school. I called her back while sitting in the back of the rescue ambulance, waiting for my partner George to restock. Just as George got into the rig to drive us back to the fire station, a man answered Daisy's phone and said, "Kay! My mom got shot!!" "Who?" I asked?

"My Mom!"

"Who got shot?" I asked for the second time, in the hopes that I would recognize the unfamiliar voice.

"My mom!" he said again...

Losing my patience, I said, "Well, who are you?!!"

"It's me, Kraig," said my nephew. His voice sounded so hoarse and anguished I didn't recognize it.

"What? Pam's been shot?" I asked.

"Yes!" Kraig answered. "Are you on your way to Cedars?"

"Why would I be going to Cedars?" I said, still trying to process the fact that my sister had been shot.

"Because that's where the paramedics said they were taking her. They said they would tell you to meet them there."

I looked at my partner and said, "George, my sister's been shot. We need to go out of service back to the station so I can get my car."

"Fuck that!!! George said, "We're going to Cedars!" He immediately got on the radio and notified O.C.D. we were out of service and needed a battalion chief and E.M.S. captain to meet us at Cedar's…

I didn't feel anything…surely if my sister were hurt badly or worse…dead, I would feel something…

I always knew when something bad happened. As a child, I was the one whom people took seriously when I called to ask my mother out of the blue, "Did anything bad happen today?" She would either be just about to pick up the phone to call me, or she would start calling around the family to find the cause for my uncomfortable feelings, knowing I was usually right. Something bad did happen!

Whenever I got that BAD FEELING, I would pray that God would protect and help whoever needed Him at that moment… and that everything would be O.K. My prayers were often answered in the way I hoped they would be, and I would immediately feel a soothing in my spirit, that my prayers were answered favorably …

I didn't feel a thing… Nothing, no feeling of dread, and now that I thought about it, I didn't feel anything when David and Maceo died in a fire either. I knew Uncle Raymond and Uncle Henry were sick, but I didn't feel it when they died. Why? I wondered, even though I was always a little afraid of this gift I was given. I felt I had some control over whatever was happening, just being able to pray about it before it was too late. So that's just what I did, started to pray for my sister as I raced to be at her bedside in the hospital. Hopefully with good news to report back to our family.

"PLEASE DEAR GOD, JEHOVAH, DON'T LET ANYTHING BAD HAPPEN TO MY SISTER. PLEASE MAKE EVERYTHING ALL RIGHT. PLEASE DON'T LET HER BE HURT BADLY. PLEASE TAKE CARE OF HER…. PLEASE TAKE CARE OF PAM. MAKE EVERYTHING OKAY." IN JESUS'S NAME, I PRAY, HELP US! AMEN (or something like this).

I waited for that comfort I always feel when I pray, and God lets me know my prayers are answered. It didn't come; I felt dread instead. I prayed again, maybe (maybe means no) I wasn't focused enough. But after I finished, still that same feeling, dread. I started to cry. George patted my hand and said, "It may not be that bad. Wait until we get to the hospital and see."

"You're right," I said. "They always call me with some kind of drama, and later, I find out it's nothing to be worried about."

Much as I tried to think good thoughts, deep inside I knew this was bad, and I knew if it was as bad as I thought it was, this was going to kill my mother. I wanted to call Pam and tell her to go and be with Mom. You must understand, whenever it came down to delivering bad news, Pam and I were always together. Whenever someone got sick and needed help, Pam and I were there together, helping out the best way we knew how. Whenever there was a tragedy, we were always there, breaking the news together, comforting together. We were so much a team anyone who talked about us would always put our names together. They would always say, Pam and Kay, Pam and Kay. Need help…you can depend on Pam and Kay.

In the middle of this thought, my phone rang. It was my husband, asking, "Where are you?"

"I'm on my way to Cedars," I said.

"Why are you going to Cedars?" I breathed a sigh of relief; it was a false alarm. He would have been the first to know if something happened to Pam. I was so glad to hear him ask me that question, but I had to make sure.

"Isn't that where they took Pam?"

He was silent for so long I had to repeat the same question. "Baby, she's gone," he said.

"What?" I said. Thinking he said she was gone… like in dead, like in, I'm all alone to take care of our family and help them deal with this horrible news. He didn't just say that, did he?

"She's gone," he repeated.

"Don't tell me that!" was all I could say over and over again until he asked me to give the phone to George.

How could my sister be dead? It couldn't be true. Somebody made a mistake! I was numb. I knew tears were falling down my face and dropping on my uniform, but I couldn't believe what my husband just said. I was still going to Cedars; I had to see my sister. I couldn't help my family with this horrible news if I couldn't believe it myself.

On my way to the hospital to see my dead sister, my phone kept ringing. Friends and family kept calling to ask me the same questions. *What happened to Pam? Is she all right?* In a fog, I answered all the questions with the information I still didn't believe myself. "PAM GOT SHOT AND SHE DIED." I had to repeat this same sentence several times because no one that called me could believe his or her ears the first time.

Why was it taking so long to get to the hospital? What route did George take?

Finally, we pulled into the parking garage of the emergency room. I saw Rescue 68 cleaning their rig, and it hit me they were the ones who brought in my sister. As I walked into Cedars, I saw her chart marked deceased. I pointed to her chart and demanded to see her. I said, "I already know. I already know. I want to see my sister." I was dressed in my turnouts, looking like I had just brought in a patient to the hospital staff, and I'm asking about the trauma patient they just pronounced dead.

People surrounded me. Nursing staff, police officers, and fire department personnel, all trying to console me. But no one would give me what I needed most! And that was to see my sister.

"Why won't you let me see my sister?" I asked.

"Her body is evidence now. You might touch her, and we can't take the chance of the evidence being destroyed." This was the answer I got!!! How could they be so mean to me? Didn't they understand I needed to see it for myself, her lifeless body! I told them they could trust me. I'd keep my hands to myself. I wouldn't touch her…I just needed to make sure they didn't have the wrong person.

I even convinced myself that I could just look at her. I know now that was a lie. If I had seen my sister lifeless, I would have started C.P.R. myself. I would have been ordering Epi and fluid replacement. I would have started IVs myself if I had to. They would have had to carry me out of there by force. I think they knew it too. They placed me in a room while waiting for the rest of my family to arrive.

Inside the room with me was the police officer who rode in the rescue with the paramedics. I started thinking about my nieces and nephew. How were they going to get through this?

Pam spoiled her kids she loved so much. Her children were so dependent on her when they were small, no one, not even our mother, wanted to babysit them when she went out for a night on the town. She was a grandmother at only forty-nine years old. Now that I thought of it, two of her grandchildren were with her, Daisy and Gregory. I asked the police officer if they were O.K. He assured me they were and that they witnessed the whole thing.

I asked him where Pam was shot. I wanted to know how this could happen to her. She was such a good person, always doing a little extra. Just to let you know how much she loved you. The police officer said Pam was getting into her car that was parked inside her parking stall when some guy tried to rob her. I asked him if anything was taken in the attempt. He said no. Then I knew it was a front for her murder. And I told him so. "My sister wasn't robbed! She has lived on that street for over ten years. Everyone on that block knows who she is...and they would never hurt her." I knew as well as I knew my name who killed her. I said, "I'll tell you exactly who shot my sister!" I related to the police officer the story of how my niece, Khristina, was robbed at gunpoint a few months back.

I told him about the threats they received afterward when she identified the robber. My sister asked for witness protection because she was afraid for her daughter's life. Detectives were assigned to the case. I said, "You need to contact them for the name of the person who robbed my niece." I didn't know Tyquan Knox's name at that time. He left me to relay that piece of information to his partner who was still at the crime scene, at Pam's apartment building. I waited for the rest of my family to arrive, not knowing what steps to take next.

If Pam were here, she would help me deal with this. How stupid of me to be thinking like this. If Pam were here, I wouldn't have this problem.

While waiting for my family, my mind ran away from me, and I didn't know how to react. Kristina and Kraig arrived first with the police. I think it was them because I remember Kristina was holding two-year-old Gregory, and he was clearly in shock, crying inconsolably.

He wanted his grandma. No one else would do!!! He never came to me on his own. Pam would always make him feel guilty by saying to him, "Give Kay-Kay some love."

This time it was I who said to him, "Come here, Baby, and give me some love." I needed love as much as he…and for the first time he reached for me without a second thought. I guess he knew she was gone, and I was the next closest person who loved her as he did.

That night as our family all gathered in my home to comfort one another, the wind blew furiously. My thoughts as I listened to Gregory cry well into the night— until I remembered to drug him with cough syrup, was…Pam is angry!!! She was as angry and as hurt as we were! I could hear her Spirit in the wind well into the night as every bed, couch, and chair was occupied by our grief! Even the floor was full of people. No one wanted to be alone with their nightmare of loss. We gathered strength from one another. As I listened to my sister's fury on the wind, I crawled into bed with my seven-year-old son and cried myself to sleep.

—⟋⟍—

Bad news travels fast. The next day more people started calling and asking what they could do to help. What do you say to people when the only thing that can make it all better is having the one who loved you back? Beautiful flowers started arriving.

Food and more people packed the house. I never thought about all the people we'd touched over the years. I never knew how much my sister was loved or how much she would be missed. I felt God had turned his back on us and didn't love me anymore. I was very angry with Him. I refused to pray to Him; after all, he didn't care about me anymore. (How mistaken I was.) People who said they would pray for us brought the most comfort because I wouldn't pray for myself.

So God sent us HIS love through all the people we had touched in some special way. People I had forgotten about. So much love by so many people. Why did God allow this to happen?

When you love something, you protect it, shield it from pain. How could He do this to us? He must be angry with me. While going through the pain, all I saw was what I lost, not all he was providing for me, for us. I can see so clearly His outpouring of love and support, now that my pain has been wiped away.

Revelations 21:1-3

1. AND I saw a new heaven and a new earth: for the first heaven and the first earth were passed away; and there was no more sea.
2. And I John saw the holy city, new Jerusalem, coming down from God out of heaven, prepared as a bride adorned for her husband.
3. And I heard a great voice out of heaven saying, Behold, the tabernacle of God is with men, and he will dwell with them, and they shall be his people, and God himself shall be with them, and be their God. *(The Holy Bible, King James Version.)*

CHAPTER 42

I Dreamed She Was An Angel

I dreamed of her death. I saw her caught unaware as the masked gunman approached her and asked for her purse. I watched her explain to the supposed robber that she didn't have anything of value, and he didn't want her empty purse. I heard her pray silently to God to spare her grandchildren. I felt her anger as she realized he really didn't want her purse at all; he came for her! I heard her thoughts as she accepted the fact that those gunshots she saw and heard fired were inside her and she was drifting away from us in death.

I HEARD HER LAST DYING THOUGHT. "HE KILLED ME! THIS CHAPTER OF MY LIFE ON EARTH IS CLOSED. MY MISSION WAS ACCOMPLISHED. I SAVED KHRISTINA. I HOPE TYQUAN LEARNS HIS LESSON WELL". ON HER FACE IS PEACE. SHE HAS PASSED TO THE NEXT LEVEL OF ANGELS ON EARTH. SOON SHE WILL BE READY TO GO HOME.

Instantly, she is transported to another place, with people she has known all her life. Briefly she remembers all the lessons she learned in her past lives, in transition to the next experience. The life when she was regally born, and when she was orphaned in Africa, and as a boy in Ireland. I am amazed, but all I can think of as I dream… is how much I miss her and how alone I am now. She looks wiser now and happy like she knows a secret and is bursting with the knowledge of it. She glanced back at me on her way to another Place and said, "Why do you miss me? You can be where I am."

I look at her in disbelief and think, I don't want to die. She laughs, like she knows something I don't, and instantly she is transported to another Place. Maybe even another time....

LIGHT

Pam (now known as Light) is floating on her back in a lake surrounded by mountains. She has had the most glorious day swimming in the lake. *The water is so warm. How can it be so warm when the sun never touches the water?* Light thinks. She watches as divers climb higher and higher, taking their lives for granted, risking their necks to break the record for the highest perfect dive. Her family was still at the Bed and Breakfast sleeping in... Her guide Tony promised to have her back in time for wine tasting. Gregory, her husband, (Shonnie's father) knows about her adventurous spirit. He knew she would be up and out before they got used to the jet lag or the time change; that's why he hired this man to be her guide. She was ready to go back, so she swam to the stone steps and climbed out of the lake.

FEARIOUS

Fearious is his name (a Viking, tall, dark and hairy, trapped in a time not his own). Fearious is trapped in a dream he can never wake up from. *How long has it been since I came to this place to raid, and where are my men? Surely, someone should be looking for me by now.* At least he is lost in a beautiful dream where he can swim, fish and hunt. The water temperature feels good. *Just one more dive and I'll break my fast. Maybe fish today...* He climbs higher than yesterday and is a little amazed as he turns around to see how small the lake looks. He briefly hopes he doesn't kill himself or break his neck as he takes a deep breath and does a perfect ten off the protruding rock!

He feels as if he is falling forever and becomes a little afraid just before he hits the water with barely a splash. Deep is his plunge. He is swimming under the water where the coolness is. After that climb, it feels wonderful.

LIGHT

Something is wrong. Light doesn't know what makes her look up as she climbs out of the water. A large man is diving off a rock that is almost at the top of the mountain. *He's going to kill himself. The lake's not deep enough to sustain a dive from that height.* Wow!!! He looks to be falling in slow motion and hits the water with barely a splash. Light can't wait to shake his hand. Fearious swims to the stone steps still in awe he is alive when a hand reaches out to help him out of the water.

"Wow!" Light says. "You are either the best diver in the world or the bravest person I've ever met. That was amazing!" Fearious looks at her hand and sees the beautiful woman it belongs to, the woman wearing the strange colorful orange garment. He thinks this dream is getting better and better…

There is something familiar about this guy. *He looks like Gregory is* Light's first thought. *Where did everyone go?* is her second. Tony! She calls… and becomes afraid when she receives no answer. "Tony!"

"Who is this Tony, your man?" says Fearious.

"No!" Light says. "My guide. Where is everyone?"

"I saw no one but you when I came out of the water," Fearious says. "I've been lost for three days and somehow I keep returning to this place. How did you get here? Where is your horse?"

"What horse? I came by car," Light says.

In my dream, Pam went on to live a new life with people she loved and knew in her other lifetimes. She had no knowledge of the life spent with me as her sister. Her life started as an adult at the age she was when she was killed. All her memories were of the life she had been transported to. With a husband named Gregory, two daughters named Shonnie and Justice and a son named Kraig. She was off to a new challenge, a new lesson to learn, and a new mission, drawing closer to God. Maybe I'll see her again in her new life when my life here is over, maybe not. Maybe this will be my last lesson to learn, and I will go home to live in heaven with the LORD FOREVER… JEHOVAH is his name.

Psalms 83:18 says, *That men may know you alone are the most high GOD.*

I do know whenever we meet again we will recognize and love each other as our journeys continue as angels on earth. I awoke feeling like she was letting me know everything is all right. She is all right, and we will be all right also… GOD had a plan for her and HE has one for US. Her favorite scripture is Jeremiah 29:11-14.

FOR I KNOW THE THOUGHTS THAT I THINK TOWARDS YOU, SAITH THE LORD, THOUGHTS OF PEACE, AND NOT OF EVIL, TO GIVE YOU AN EXPECTED END. THEN SHALL YE CALL UPON ME, AND YE SHALL GO AND PRAY UNTO ME, AND I WILL HEARKEN UNTO YOU. AND YE SHALL SEEK ME, AND FIND ME, WHEN YE SHALL SEARCH FOR ME WITH ALL YOUR HEART. AND I WILL BE FOUND OF YOU, SAITH THE LORD: AND I WILL TURN AWAY YOUR CAPTIVITY.

AND I WILL GATHER YOU FROM ALL THE NATIONS, AND FROM ALL THE PLACES WHITHER I HAVE DRIVEN YOU, SAITH THE LORD; AND I WILL BRING YOU AGAIN INTO THE PLACE WHENCE I CAUSED YOU TO BE CARRIED AWAY CAPTIVE.

CHAPTER 43

Over a Year Later

DE'CHANNE LANE
OCTOBER 9, 2008

From tragedy to triumph, how long does it take to think of something you have experienced that is life-changing? If one must scuffle with one's brain to identify a turning point in one's life, then is it truly and undeniably life-changing? Maybe you were just moved for that brief moment and it made you inquisitive for a meager amount of time. Immediately when I think of a life-changing experience, only one thing comes to mind. I cannot say I was exactly thrilled to go into depth about it, so I tried to think of another incident. It soon became clear to me that writing my first poem was not exactly life-changing. My grandmother's murder was.

It was the morning of January 4, 2007, and I had spent the night at my grandmother's apartment in Los Angeles, CA. Our Internet at home was down, so I had ridden home with my grandma, hoping for the chance to get on Myspace and check my email. My plans were to get up early and go with my aunt, Khristina, to Santa Monica College, and use the library computers while she was in class. I awoke, however, to find that things this morning were going to be completely off track for what I had planned. By the time I finally got up, Khrissy had already left for school, not to mention I woke up with a bloodstain on my grandmother's cover. Great, I thought to myself, this is all I need right now.

Knowing my grandma, being the obsessively compulsive neat freak that she was, would have a fit, I threw the cover in the dirty clothes hamper. I told myself when I had time I would go back and wash them before she could find out. I then went into the room with my uncle, Kraig, deciding to watch TV with him until Khris got out of class.

Soon after, my grandma and my two-year-old brother, Greg, came into the room. My grandma sat on the edge of the bed I was on, and Greg sat on the floor hugging a doll he got for Christmas. Kraig made a big deal about this doll and told my grandma they were going to come home and find the doll missing. They joked around for a while about the doll that Greg was holding onto ever so tightly. He seemed so content sitting there with his doll, and even though I didn't approve of a boy having a doll, it didn't make him any less masculine to hold it. Actually, in my eyes, it made him seem even more innocent.

As always, Kraig and his mother, my grandma, start arguing. She was mad at him for not washing the dishes or taking out the trash. One of her biggest pet peeves was having to go to sleep with dirty dishes in the sink. This used to amuse me because she acted as if the dishes were going to come to life overnight and attack us. That was my grandma though, and it was one of the things that made her who she was. Kraig started getting on her about why she never made Khris do anything as if she was a baby. He felt as if she always took her side no matter what the argument was about. I sat looking at the both of them, unfocused until I heard her say, "Please, Kraig, I don't have much time."

This statement caught me off guard, and I wondered what made her say that? Why would she start talking as if she were leaving or something? My mind began to race as I wondered, *What would our life be like if she left us?* Being the sheltered girl that I was, I never had to experience the real world because my family had always protected me from reality. I can remember sucking on my two fingers while playing with my grandma's bracelets. Even though I was only one year younger than my aunt, she was interested in boys at a much earlier age than me. I was just too shy and didn't have any confidence. Today, they could not protect me any longer, as reality unsheathed itself and introduced the real world to a seventeen-year-old, De'Channe Lane. As it was getting close to the time Khris got out of school, my grandma asked Kraig, since he was picking up his girlfriend from the same school, if he could get Khris also. He started going on and on about how much that would inconvenience him. His first argument was that he didn't want to have to wait for her and try to find her. Then he started talking about having to take his girl to the YMCA for their field trip that day. My grandma asked if he could take her with him and she would just pick her up from the YMCA since it was closer. Kraig still insisted that it would be better if she just picked Khris up, so we all made our way out. Kraig was the first to leave. I remember my grandma and I watched as he pulled out of the gates.

It so happened that even though she told Kraig to take out the trash, she was the one that ended up doing it. She walked to the dumpster and I played around with Greg. As I was holding him, he dropped his doll. Pointlessly reaching for it, as if his arms were long enough, he started to whine as I continued teasing him. My grandma came to the rescue of her grandson and walked over to pick up his doll as I waited by the car for her. She walked over and opened the door; I turned around and faced the wall. I don't remember exactly why I turned to face the wall at this moment; maybe it was to tease my brother even more since he was still reaching for his doll.

I turned around to see this tall, black male with all black sweats, a hood, and a black rag covering his face up to his nose facing my grandma. He had this BB gun pointed at her and I wondered, *What is Thomas doing?* Thomas was their neighbor and I figured he and my grandma were messing around.

This was just another one of her pranks she always pulled. My grandma was so full of life and was always going on with these corny pranks and jokes. He asked for her purse, and she replied simply, telling him that there was nothing inside of it. There was a pause that seemed to last forever even though it was probably a millisecond as he stared with his eyes darting back from her to me. When he looked at me, it was with uncertainty as if he could see me, but I wasn't there. My grandma, however, didn't look at me once. It was as if, if she looked at me, it would confirm my whereabouts.

He asked again for her purse, and she held up her hand as if telling him to stop or pause and replied, "Please, sir, there's nothing in it." Next thing I know there were four bangs and smoke everywhere as my eyes watched him run away. My grandma fell like a scene out of a movie, her body sliding slowly but gracefully down the side of the car onto the floor. Her arms fell limp at her sides, and her head tilted to one side. She had Greg's doll in one hand and her purse in the other. Everything was silent as I stood there, not moving an inch, waiting for her to get up and the guy to come back, and for them to start laughing. This was not a very good joke, I thought, still waiting. I saw blood running down the side of her neck, and I felt something inside of me turn. I am not a religious person, but I could no longer feel her presence, and as much as I didn't want to believe it, she was gone.

This was no joke, and that was no BB gun. How could this happen? She was so calm. I didn't sense anything wrong with the situation, and it was all too surreal. Why? Why didn't she tell us something or say something to us so we could have known what was going on? As he stared from her to me I wondered to myself if she did that to protect us? So many thoughts start rushing through my head, and I just started to run.

Without thinking about where I was going, my feet carried me to the balcony above my grandma's apartment and I sat there, crying, while rocking Greg back and forth in my arms. I held him tightly as tears fell down my face. I started to hate myself for leaving my grandma there, but I didn't know what to do. What if she was still alive and I just left her there? What if she died because of me? I should have helped her. When I saw him I should have screamed.

Maybe I took too long to get into the car because I was too busy messing with Greg, and I always made her do everything. There I was again being a bad grandchild and never helping out my grandma. All I ever did was give her attitude, and now she was gone, forever. I would never see her again.

I got my cell phone and tried to call 911, but every time I called, the line was busy. I cried even harder, unaware of the people staring or anything until I saw my uncle's car pull back up. He knows, I told myself as I screamed his name. The music was too loud, and he stood there looking for who was calling his name, or if he was mistaken. The look on his face told me I was wrong, and he didn't know anything. He was innocent. I screamed his name again, and he finally looked up. "Somebody shot Grandma!" I choked out and he just stared at me with confusion. It's hard to ever believe anyone if they told you that. Who would kill a woman like her? I repeated myself and he asked me where was she? I pointed to the back and ran down the stairs, happy to have someone with me. Maybe he could tell me what was going on and then everything would be okay.

As I made my way to the back, I saw his expression as he saw his mother lying in her own blood, lifeless. It was as if he tripped on air and fell on his knees, quickly picking himself up as he tried to find his equilibrium. He took his hat off. I saw his face covered in tears as if he had been slapped in the face by this devastating truth. His face no longer had that innocence of the bliss he once had as this scene stood before him.

"Daisy, you have to stay here with my mom, please, stay here with her. I have to go get Sammie and Khris. Stay here with her, please; I don't want to leave my mom alone." He was so hurt I could hear it in his voice as the tears kept coming. I stared at him. Seeing my uncle broken down like this really hurt me; he was always so strong. It was strange to me how he was begging that I stay with her, as if I would leave. He sped out of the gates as he rushed to go pick up Khris and Sammie.

I remember calling everyone I knew, but no one would pick up. I finally got in touch with my Uncle Al and tried to tell him what happened. It was as if I were speaking a foreign language because he couldn't understand a word I was saying. When he finally heard me, everything was silent. It was as if he dropped the phone. Then he failed to hide his cries as he told me everything would be okay and that they were on their way. My Uncle Michael was there; he was a detective for the LAPD. I hung up the phone as police began showing up. I don't even remember calling them, but they were there. They start questioning me as I sat on the steps with Greg in my lap.

He was quiet; I actually can't remember him making one noise since my grandmother was shot.

Everybody started turning up, crying, devastated, and standing around. The presence of my family made me feel safe. Khris had finally gotten there and started screaming and running trying to get to my grandma, but they wouldn't let her. It was like a scene out of a movie. Everything seemed scripted. I don't even want to go into detail about the events that followed that day. Me, walking out of the detective's office after being separated from my family for hours.

Finally walking into the room to see everyone seated at the tables. Hurt on everyone's faces. It was uncomfortable walking in as all eyes fell upon me. Everything went into slow motion as my mother ran up to me and hugged me, crying. As much as I tried to stay strong, I fell apart in her arms. Everyone around us disappeared, and although I am sure they were crying, I could no longer see them. It was hard for everyone to believe that this could have happened. My grandma was such a great woman, and she touched the lives of everyone. When we had her funeral, it was closed casket because my mother didn't want anyone to see her like that. They had stuffed cotton in her ears because she had received a gunshot through her ears, two in her side, and one in her hand, as she held it up in defense. The church was packed, and there were even people gathering outside to get a look in. It was a good thing no one got to see her; it took so long for the coroner's office to finish with her body that there was no more color in her. My grandma was forty-nine years old and a very light-skinned woman. She looked young yet her body now was darker than mine and wrinkly. The lipstick on her lips just made her look even worse; it made her lips look like a dried-out rose. Sometimes I think Kraig and I were the lucky ones because although we saw her covered in blood, she still looked like herself and full of life. The few that got to see my grandmother at the wake were left with the image of an old dried-out imposter. I wish I could say that this experience changed me for the better, but I can't exactly admit that. It is true that I am starting to figure out who De'Channe Lane is, but the cost is high. I find myself going in circles, confused. I am distant, and I don't open myself up to the ones closest to me. I find myself longing for love because I never want to be alone again like I was on that day. I can say that my grandma taught me to stay strong and to be brave. Up to the very moment she died she instilled that quality in me. I love her forever, and I wish I could tell her how much. I know I never really appreciated her before, but if I could have her back, I would show her. I would hold onto her forever so that she could never go anywhere again. I also find myself having trouble believing in religion. I question the faith of my family, distancing us even further.

I understand that I could have easily died that day at the hands of Tyquan Knox, but I am still here. For my grandmother, I will live, and I will be appreciative of my life. Even though she was poor, you could never tell she was unhappy because she wasn't. She lived for us, and we made her life complete. I understand that now. I used to be sheltered, but now I have a very close relationship with reality and the many hardships my family has faced since the death of Pamala Sue Lark.

This was my life-changing experience. It was so easy to realize that. I did not have to scuffle with my mind to confirm this. That is because I know in my heart this is the one thing that altered my life. It is as if everything before that day didn't exist as I now struggle while memories of her slip away. I think about her sometimes, when I am alone, and cry. I cry to myself because I do not want anyone else to feel my pain. No one but me should have to live with what it has done to me and the person that I am. I hope one day I can make her proud. One thing I can say is that she has taught me to see good in everyone. I give every single person the benefit of the doubt; sometimes I put those below me before myself and go out of my way to make them happy. I know if she were able to talk to me, she wouldn't want me to hate her killer. She died for a reason because if it wasn't her, it would have been Khris, the intended victim. My grandma died for her; she died for us, all of my family. I appreciate that. They say behind every great person is a struggle, and I am still struggling. I am not perfect by far. This is my life, from tragedy to triumph.

CHAPTER 44

The Trial

DAY ONE
OPENING STATEMENTS
DANETTE MYRESS (D.A.)

The D.A. started off telling the story of how four teenagers were victims of a robbery in September of 2006 and how the defendant was identified by one of the victims by name. She said that Khristina Henry was afraid to report the crime, but her mother compelled her to do the right thing. She painted the picture of how Khristina Henry was in fear after receiving threats and intimidation from the mother and friends of the defendant. She explained to the jury that Khristina and her mother asked for help and protection from the Los Angeles Police Department due to that fear. She described how Kristina's mother was killed in her parking area four days before the court date for the robber and of the defendant's girlfriend's involvement. She explained that the finger was pointed at the killer of Pamala Lark by the girlfriend of the defendant, who was caught driving the getaway car, and how her role as accomplice would have given her a life sentence without possibility of parole. She described how the girlfriend was offered a plea bargain for her complete and truthful testimony. She ended with the statement that all the evidence would point to the defendant beyond a reasonable doubt!

DEFENDANT'S LAWYERS
SWEENEY & POWELL

Mr. Sweeney started off by telling the jury to empty their cup and taste his tea. (This was his effort to wipe their minds of the D.A.'s words.) He went on to say that the accomplice would say anything to save herself. He called her a liar and talked about how madly in love she was with the defendant. He told the jury the defendant's career as a football player was in its budding stages, and the girlfriend had a dream of becoming his wife. He talked about how she was caught in bed with the defendant and how he was beaten up by her uncles, one of whom was a Rollin 40's Crip. He described her love for the defendant and her two abortions. He told the jury that she was the mastermind of the killing because, after all… she was the smart one. She had a 4.0 grade-point average and was offered a full ride to college. She had the brains and motivation because of her love. He talked about how her father and mother wanted to get her away from the defendant so desperately that they took her car away. The Defense stated, "When she left home to go and live with the defendant, she was so jealous, the mother of the defendant had to put her out." He painted a picture of fear of her father after he beat her beyond recognition and claimed that that was why she was framing the defendant for this murder. He told the jury he would prove the defendant had an alibi on the night of the robbery in September when the Rollin 40's Crips were robbing the kids at the bowling alley.

He said the defendant was a well-known football player and this was a case of mistaken identity. He said he would show how the victim's mother called the mother of the defendant three times because they had a friendly relationship. He said he would show that the brother-in-law of the victim (Michael Slider) led the L.A.P.D. in the wrong direction when he showed up on the crime scene saying, "I know who did it! Tyquan Knox." This act by Michael Slider resulted in other evidence ignored and other suspects not pursued. He said he had proof that another person committed the crime, a person named Justin. He said the witnesses saw a man dressed all in black running from the scene. The man was 6' 4" in height, while the defendant is

5' 11". He stated the girlfriend of the defendant was kept awake for twenty-four hours and was pressured into pointing the finger at the defendant by the L.A.P.D. and her parents.

He said her obsession with the defendant was so intense she needed psychiatric help. He stated that he would prove by the defendant's cellphone records that the girlfriend lied when she said she woke the defendant up at 0530 hours to commit the crime. He said the evidence taken from the crime scene—coffee cup and paper sleeve, bloody footprints—as well as no gunshot residue found on the defendant would make it clear he was not guilty.

THE D.A. MYRES REQUESTED DISCOVERY (10-27-09)

1. Jealous rage
2. Beating of girlfriend beyond recognition.
3. False statement about gunshot residue.
4. L.A.P.D. failure to investigate other suspects.
5. Witnesses statement about a 6'4" man in black.
6. Witness at the bowling alley

The judge reminded the jury that these statements by the defense lawyer were not evidence and the jury should wait for the evidence.

CHAPTER 45

Day 2 of Court 10-27-09

WITNESS #1
KHRISTINA HENRY
D.A. MEYERS

ON 9-3-06 WHAT HAPPENED?
Khristina talked about how she and some friends started out the evening at a restaurant called P.F. Chang's to celebrate the birthday of Ebonie White. She said they all went back to her house to drop off one of the cars before going bowling. They got to the bowling alley and bowled for about two hours before leaving at around midnight. Upon leaving the bowling alley, she saw a young man she knew from middle school, named Ryan Betton, who called her name and said, "Hi." She noticed he was standing in a crowd of about ten other teenagers. As she opened the door to the car and threw in her purse, she saw a young man pointing a gun at her boyfriend, Donovan Diaz.

DO YOU SEE THE GUNMAN IN THE COURTROOM TODAY?
"Yes," she said and pointed to the defendant, Tyquan Knox. "He was the one who approached Donovan and robbed him. He said, 'What you got?' Then pulled a gun out and cocked it. He said, 'I'll shoot you right now.' That's when I noticed a second man at the rear of the car saying, 'We want sidekicks and cell

phones, all of that.' Ebonie and Amber were in the process of getting into the car when the robbery occurred. After the robbery, Tyquan and the other man returned to the group standing in front of the bowling alley."

The victims drove away and called the police, who directed them to return to the bowling alley. They were afraid to go back and went home instead. Khristina then called her mother, Pamala Lark, who was not home at the time. Donovan spent the night, and the next day Pamala Lark took them to the police station to report the crime. Khristina heard the name of the robber from Ebonie or Amber when they were in the car after the robbery. Approximately one week later she was called into the police station to look at a six-pack of pictures, to I.D. the robber.

WHAT HAPPENED AFTER THE ROBBERY THAT CAUSED YOU CONCERN?

"I started receiving phone calls (cell) from Tyquan's mother. She said she was calling to find out what happened. She said the police were looking for her son and that he said he didn't rob any girl. She wanted to know what she could do to make it all go away. She asked my mom how much money it would cost her.

"My mother said, 'If he had killed my daughter, would you be calling and asking what you could do to make it all go away?' My mother reported this call to the police, to a detective named Vittraino, the next day. The defendant's mother called back approximately a week later and said her son wanted to talk to my mother and she would call right back after she arrived at her son's location. About an hour later she called back and put him on the phone. He told my mother that he saw what happened, but he didn't commit the robbery. My mother told him, "Then, baby, you don't have anything to worry about." Then she hung up the phone.

"I started receiving text messages next and again reported this to the police, a Detective Vittranio."

WHAT HAPPENED ON 12-11-06 AT PRE-LIM FOR ROBBERY?

Khristina said she went to the courthouse at the airport location and saw the defendants there in the hallway, after learning the preliminary hearing had been canceled. She knew the defendant's girlfriend from the MySpace website. Khristina also became afraid when the defendant's girlfriend came to her place of employment, at the Coffee Bean, and ordered a drink. She called her mother and also reported this incident to the police detective.

WHAT HAPPENED ON January 4, 2007?
"I went to school, to Santa Monica. Kraig and Sammie drove me. My mother was alive when I left for school."

HOW DID YOU I.D. MR. KNOX AFTER THE ROBBERY?
"I said he was 6' 0" tall and was wearing dark clothes, maybe red shorts."

DID YOU DESCRIBE THE GUN?
"I don't know."

6-25-07 AT THE PRE-LIM HEARING DID YOU I.D. TYQUAN KNOX?
"Yes."

ARE YOU POSITIVE ABOUT HIS INVOLVEMENT IN THE ROBBERY?
"Yes."

Cross-examination (Mr. Sweeney)

WAS A SECURITY GUARD AT THE DOOR REFUSING TO LET ANYONE ELSE INSIDE THE BOWLING ALLEY?
"I don't know."

HOW DO YOU KNOW RYAN BETTON?
"I went to Webster Middle School with him."

WAS RYAN WITH ANYONE?

"He was with a group of people."

HOW FAR AWAY WAS THE CAR FROM THE DOOR OF BOWLING ALLEY?
"About forty-five to fifty feet away."

WHO GOT INSIDE THE CAR?
"I'm not sure."

DID YOU TELL THE POLICE HIS SHORTS WERE RED OR DARK?
"I'm not sure."

WHEN WAS THE LAST TIME YOU TALKED TO THE D.A.?
"Monday, a week ago."

DID THE ROBBER HAVE ON A HAT, BEANIE OR A CAP?
"I don't know."

DID HE HAVE A FADE HAIRCUT?
"I don't know."

WHERE DID THE GUN COME FROM?
"I'm not sure, maybe his waistband."

WERE YOU STARING AT THE GUN?
"No."

DID YOU SAY IT WAS A BLUE STEEL TYPE OF GUN?
"No."

DID YOU SEE THE TOP HALF OF THE GUN PULLED BACK?
"Yes, he cocked the gun."

WHERE WAS RYAN?
"I don't know."

DO YOU KNOW KEISHA BROOKS?
"No."

DID YOU SEE RYAN WITH ANYONE?
"Yes, a group of people."

DID YOU SEE RYAN WITH A GIRL?
"No."

WHEN WAS THE FIRST TIME YOU ALL TALKED ABOUT THE ROBBERY?
"In the car. Ebonie may have said it was Tyquan because she went to school with him and knew who he was."

DONAVON PLAYED FOOTBALL. DID YOU GO TO THE GAMES?
"No."

DID YOU GOOGLE TYQUAN AFTER THE ROBBERY?
"No."

EVER?
"Yes."

ISN'T IT TRUE YOU GOOGLED HIM RIGHT AFTER YOU GOT ROBBED?
"No."

HOW LONG DID IT TAKE YOU TO I.D. TYQUAN IN THE PHOTO LINEUP?
"Two minutes although I knew who he was right away."

YOU WROTE ON THE LINEUP PICTURE, "HE HAS A FAMILIAR FACE, LOOKS LIKE THE GUY WITH THE GUN." CORRECT?

"Yes."

NOT 'THAT'S HIM.' AND YOU COULD HAVE WRITTEN ANYTHING YOU WANTED, CORRECT?

"Yes."

DID TYQUAN'S MOTHER THREATEN YOU WITH WORDS?

"No."

WAS SHE JUST A CONCERNED PARENT WHEN SHE CALLED YOU?

"Yes, you can say that."

YOU FELT THREATENED BY THE CALL, BUT SHE DIDN'T SAY WATCH YOUR BACK?

"No."

SHE WAS CONCERNED ABOUT HER SON'S FOOTBALL CAREER, CORRECT?

"Yes, she said he had been in trouble before, and this could be bad for his football career."

YOUR MOTHER CALLED CARLA KNOX SEVERAL TIMES, CORRECT?

"No. Not to my knowledge."

KEEIARRA DASHIELL CAME INTO THE COFFEE BEAN AND STARED AT YOU AND MADE YOU FEEL UNCOMFORTABLE, DIDN'T SHE?

"Yes."

TYQUAN WASN'T WITH HER, WAS HE?
"Not in the store."

IN THE AIM FROM RYAN, HE SAID TYQUAN DIDN'T ROB YOU, DIDN'T HE?
"Yes."

KEEIARRA CAME INTO THE COFFEE BEAN AND ORDERED A DRINK NOT ON THE MENU, CORRECT?
"Yes."

DID YOU ASK A FRIEND NAMED MATT IF HE GAVE OUT YOUR PHONE NUMBER?
"Yes. And he said yes."

DID YOU GIVE A STATEMENT TO THE POLICE AFTER YOUR MOTHER WAS KILLED?
"I don't remember."
She is handed a written statement to refresh her memory. It said Khristina heard Keeiarra was looking for her from another person.

DID YOU TELL THE POLICE KEEIARRA DROVE A CHAMPAGNE ULTIMA, AND TYQUAN ALWAYS DROVE HER CAR?
"No."

DID YOU SEE A ULTIMA AT THE BOWLING ALLEY?
"No."

ON 1-4-07, WHAT TIME DID YOU LEAVE THE HOUSE?
"At about 7:30 am."

HOW DID YOU FIND OUT KEEIARRA WAS TYQUAN'S GIRLFRIEND?
"Brian told me."

DID KEEIARRA LOOK AT YOU ON 12-11-06?
"Yes."

(Re-direct) D.A. Meyers

DID YOU SEE TYQUAN AT THE HEARING ON 12-11-06?
"Yes."

WAS HE DRESSED IN PRISON GARB OR IN STREET CLOTHES?
"He was dressed in street clothes."

DID YOUR MOTHER AGREE TO TAKE MONEY FROM CARLA KNOX TO MAKE IT ALL GO AWAY?
"No."

DID YOU FEEL THREATENED AND ASK FOR RELOCATION TO MOVE?
"Yes."

WERE THE CONDITIONS THE SAME AS THIS PICTURE WHEN YOU WERE ROBBED? (Khristina is shown a picture of the bowling alley, showing it as well lit.)
"Yes.

WHEN DID YOU GOOGLE TYQUAN KNOX?
"After my mother's death."

WHAT TIME WAS YOUR CLASS?
"I don't remember."

HOW LONG DOES IT TAKE TO GET TO S.M. COLLEGE?
"About twenty minutes."

Cross-examination of direct (Mr. Sweeney)

DID YOU FEEL THREATENED BY TEXT MESSAGES AND PHONE CALLS?
"Yes."

NONE OF THOSE SIX IMPLIED THREATS CAME FROM TYQUAN, CORRECT?
"Correct."

DID YOU SEE THE LIGHTS ON AT THE BOWLING ALLEY?
"Yes because the light was coming from that direction."

DID YOU EVER TELL THE POLICE THAT THE ROBBERS HAD LEFT THE SCENE?
"Not that I remember."

Re-direct (D.A. Meyers)

ALL THE THREATS WERE BECAUSE OF THE ROBBERY, CORRECT?
"Yes."

Cross-examination of direct (Mr. Sweeney)

NONE OF THOSE THREATS CAME FROM TYQUAN, CORRECT?
"Correct."

(NO MORE QUESTIONS AT THIS TIME)

10-27-09
WITNESS #2, DONOVAN DIAZ

Donovan talked about the same things that Khristina had testified to starting with the group going from P. F. Chang's to Khristina's house and the bowling alley. He said they left P.F. Chang's around 7:00 P.M., arriving at the bowling alley around 9:30-10:00, and they stayed for about one and a half hours, leaving before midnight. He confirmed Khristina's story. He stated he was robbed by Tyquan at gunpoint with a silver automatic handgun of two hundred dollars, a gold Rolex chain, and his wallet. He said Tyquan was wearing a beanie, t-shirt, and shorts at the time of the robbery. He stated he went to the police station with Pam and Christina the next day to report the crime. He was shown a six-pack of pictures and I.D.'d Tyquan on 11-03-06. He wrote under the six-pack, "I'm positive it was # 5." He said there were three of them altogether.

On the day of the pre-lim, he saw Tyquan in the hall of the court building. He said he was threatened before Pam was killed. This happened around 1-1-07.

Cross-examination (Mr. Sweeney)

HOW MANY PEOPLE WERE OUTSIDE OF THE BOWLING ALLEY?
"Maybe seven. I don't recall ten to twenty."

DID KHRISTINA TALK TO RYAN?
"Not that I recall."

WHERE DID THE MEN COME FROM THAT ROBBED YOU?
"Thirty yards away."

WAS IT DARK?
"Yes."

DID KHRISTINA GET INTO THE CAR?
"No, she opened the door."
WHERE DID THE ROBBERS COME FROM?
"I don't recall."

COULD THEY HAVE COME FROM LINCOLN BL.?
"Yes."

ON 6-25-07, AT THE ARRAIGNMENT HEARING, DO YOU RECAL THESE STATEMENTS? CAN YOU TELL THE COURT WHAT OCCURRED TO YOU? HOW MANY PEOPLE CAME BEHIND YOU?
"Maybe three or four. One pulled a gun."

AND WHAT COLOR WAS THE T-SHIRT OF THE GUY WHO ROBBED YOU? WAS IT A LIGHT COLOR?"
"No, it was dark."
(In the record of 6-25-07, Donovan stated the color of the shirt was white.)

WHAT COLOR WERE THE SHORTS?
"I believe they were basketball shorts."

WHERE WAS THE GUN PULLED FROM?
Waist area."

WHAT COLOR WERE THEY? DID YOU SAY THEY WERE RED?
"I don't know, no."

WHERE WAS AMBER?
"In the car."

AND EBONIE SAID SHE SAW TYQUAN BEFORE, CORRECT?
"Yes."

WHAT POSITION DID YOU PLAY IN FOOTBALL?
"Outside linebacker. My job was to tackle anyone with the ball."

DID YOU PLAY CRENSHAW?
"Yes, in 2005."

WERE YOU A STRONG SAFETY?
"I played Strong Safety before."

DID YOU KNOW TYQUAN KNOX?
"No!"

(The defense tries to make it look like Donovan should have known Tyquan because he was an up-and-coming famous football player.)

HAVE YOU EVER GOOGLED TYQUAN?
"No."

HOW LONG DID IT TAKE YOU TO PICK TYQUAN OUT OF A LINEUP?
"A millisecond."

BECAUSE YOU KNEW HIM BEFORE BEING ROBBED, CORRECT?
"No."
(Threat was in the context; you better watch your back.)

Re-direct (D.A. Meyers)

WAS YOUR MEMORY BETTER ON 9-03-06 WHEN YOU MADE YOUR POLICE REPORT?
"Yes."

WAS IT BETTER ON 6-25-07 AT THE ARRAIGNMENT HEARING?

"Yes."

D.A. Meyers gives Donovan the police report to review to refresh his memory, then asked him:

HOW MANY PEOPLE APPROACHED YOU ON THIS REPORT?
"Two."

WHAT WAS THE PERSON WEARING WHO ROBBED YOU?
"Black clothing and red shorts."

ARE YOU POSITIVE TYQUAN ROBBED YOU?
"Yes."

HAVE YOU EVER PLAYED FOOTBALL WITH TYQUAN KNOX?
"No."

DO YOU KNOW ANY MEMBERS OF THE CRENSHAW FOOTBALL TEAM?
"No."

Cross-examination (Mr. Sweeney)

WHO IS SEQUOIA? DID HER BOYFRIEND PLAY FOOTBALL FOR CRENSHAW?
"Sequoia told me to watch my back. I didn't know her boyfriend like that."

DID YOU MAKE YOUR POLICE REPORT TO THE FRONT DESK OF THE POLICE STATION?
"Yes."

WHO SPOKE FIRST AT THE POLICE STATION, KHRISTINA, HER MOTHER, OR YOU?
"Her mother, me, then Khristina."

YOU SWORE TO TELL THE TRUTH ON 6-25-07, NOT AT THE POLICE STATION, RIGHT?
"Yes."

Re-direct (D.A. Meyers)

ARE YOU TELLING THE TRUTH? YOU'RE NOT LYING TO THE COURT, ARE YOU?
"Yes. No."

10-27-09 (D.A. MEYERS)
WITNESS #3, AMBER MIZE

Amber talked about going to Khristina's house to drop off her car. This happened just after the birthday party for Ebonie at P.F. Chang's. She stated they left the bowling alley after midnight. She also stated that Tyquan was the robber. She said he asked Donovan, "What you got?" and she heard a handgun being cocked. She said all of them were standing outside the car, getting ready to get in when the robbery occurred. She saw Tyquan take Khristina's phone and hand it to another man. She confirmed the accounts by Khristina and Donovan of what happened after leaving the scene of the bowling alley. She said the robber had on a cap or hat and was wearing a black shirt.

WHEN DID YOU REPORT THE ROBBERY?
"I'm not sure. I went with Khristina to the police station."

DO YOU NEED GLASSES TO SEE?
"Yes, far away."

HOW MANY PEOPLE WERE OUTSIDE THE BOWLING ALLEY?

"Maybe ten, wearing white t-shirts and around eighteen years of age."

DID YOU TALK TO THE DETECTIVE AT THE POLICE STATION?

"Yes, with Khristina. I picked out #5 in the six-pack. I said, 'I definitely
saw his face before; he was the guy who had the gun.'"

HAVE YOU EVER SEEN TYQUAN BEFORE?

"No."

(Break for the day)

CHAPTER 46

10-28-09
Day Three of the Trial

(D.A. Meyers)

ON 12-11-06, THE AIRPORT COURTHOUSE, DID YOU SEE TYQUAN IN THE HALLWAY? WHEN YOU WERE WITH PAMALA LARK AND KHRISTINA?
"Yes."

AT THE PRELIMINARY HEARING OF 6-25-07, DID YOU I.D. TYQUAN KNOX?
"Yes."

ARE YOU POSITIVE IT WAS TYQUAN THAT TOOK DONOVAN'S PROPERTY?
"Yes."

WHEN YOU GOT INTO THE CAR DO YOU REMEMBER EBONIE SAYING IT WAS TYQUAN THAT ROBBED DONOVAN?
"I don't remember."

DID YOU TELL KHRISTINA WHO YOU PICKED IN THE SIX-PACK LINEUP?
"No."

Cross-examination (Mr. Sweeney)

HAVE YOU EVER SEEN MR. KNOX BEFORE 09-03-06?
"No."

ARE YOU POSITIVE?
"Yes."

DO YOU REMEMBER BEING AT A PARTY AT RICKY'S HOUSE, WHERE TYQUAN WAS PRESENT?
"No."

DO YOU REMEMBER AN INCIDENT WHEN SOMEONE LOCKED YOU OUT OF YOUR CAR, AND YOU BANGED ON THE CAR TO GET IN?
"Yes, I remember the incident."

THAT WAS TYQUAN INSIDE YOUR CAR, RIGHT?
"I don't remember."

DO YOU REMEMBER WHO WAS IN YOUR CAR?
"No, I just said get out of my car."

DID YOU TALK TO EBONIE AFTER THE ROBBERY?
"No."

KHRISTINA, HOW MANY TIMES?
"Yes, we talked once."

DID TYQUAN'S NAME COME UP WHEN YOU TALKED?
"No."

WHEN WAS THE FIRST TIME HIS NAME CAME UP?
"In 2006, when I was ordered to court."

ON YOUR DRIVE TO COURT DID YOU TALK ABOUT
TYQUAN?
"Yes."

Re-direct (D.A. Meyers)

WHEN YOU WERE UNDER OATH, DID YOU EVER
SEE TYQUAN BEFORE THE ROBBERY?
"I said no, I don't know him. I don't know if he was in my car."

WHERE WAS EBONIE'S CAR PARKED ON THE NIGHT
OF THE ROBBERY?
"Across from the bowling alley."

Cross-examination of re-direct (Mr. Sweeney)

DO YOU KNOW RYAN BETTON?
"No."

DID YOU GO AND ASK ANYONE AT THE PARTY WHO
THE GUYS WERE WHO WERE IN YOUR CAR?
"No."

10-28-09 (D.A. MEYERS)
(WITNESS #4) EBONIE WHITE

Ebonie talked about her birthday party at P.F. Chang's that started at 6 P.M. and lasted about three hours. She followed Khristina and Donovan to her house and drove everyone to the bowling alley. They stayed until around closing time, around 12:00 A.M to 12:30 A.M. She never got into the car while Donovan was being robbed. She noticed two men behind her robbing Donovan. She identified

Tyquan as the one with the gun. She couldn't see what was happening to Khristina with the other man. She said after the robbery, they left the scene, and Khristina called the police while still inside the car.

WHAT DID YOU SAY IN THE CAR?
"I said that was Tyquan who robbed us."

WHAT WAS TYQUAN WEARING?
"I don't know."

She was shown a picture of the parking lot of the bowling alley and was asked where she parked. She was unsure where she parked. Ebonie was also shown a six-pack of photos and picked Tyquan, # 5 bottom middle. She wrote under the picture, "That's the guy who pulled the gun on my friend. I know him from Crenshaw High School." This was her first time testifying in court

Cross-examination (Mr. Sweeney)

RICKY COLLINS IS YOUR BOYFRIEND, CORRECT?
"Yes."

YOUR BOYFRIEND WAS A FOOTBALL PLAYER AT CRENSHAW, CORRECT?
"Yes."

HOW MANY TIMES HAVE YOU SEEN TYQUAN?
"About three times. I went to summer school and saw him with other football players."

WAS KHRISTINA OR AMBER EVER WITH YOU WHEN YOU SAW TYQUAN WITH OTHER FOOTBALL PLAYERS?
"No."

HOW MANY TIMES HAVE YOU SEEN TYQUAN ALTOGETHER?
"Maybe five times, but I never talked to him."

HOW MANY TIMES HAVE YOU, AMBER AND KHRISTINA BEEN TOGETHER AND SEEN TYQUAN?
"Maybe twice."

YOU AND AMBER WERE AT RICKY'S HOUSE, AND TYQUAN WAS THERE, CORRECT?
"Yes."

DID YOU KNOW ANY OF THE MEN IN THE GROUP STANDING OUTSIDE THE BOWLING ALLEY?
"No."

DID YOU LOOK AROUND TO SEE IF YOU KNEW ANYONE?
"No."

WHAT MADE YOU TURN AROUND?
"I heard a commotion behind me and noticed Donovan being robbed by Tyquan."

WHEN YOU GOT INTO THE CAR, WHAT DID YOU SAY TO YOUR FRIENDS?
"I said that was Tyquan that robbed us."

WHAT DID KHRISTINA SAY?
"She said, 'They took my phone.'"

ON 9-25-06, THE FIRST TIME YOU WENT TO THE POLICE STATION, DID YOU KNOW TYQUAN'S LAST NAME?
"No."

WHO DID YOU TALK TO DURING THOSE TWENTY-TWO DAYS BEFORE GOING TO THE POLICE STATION?
"No one I can recall besides my mother."

DID AMBER OR KHRISTINA SAY IT WAS T̶
WHEN YOU GOT INTO THE CAR?
"No, I was the only one."

(Re-direct) D.A. Meyers

DID YOU KNOW IF DONOVAN OR KHRISTINA
REPORTED THE INCIDENT TO THE POLICE?
"No. I knew two weeks before I went to the police because I
needed to talk to them. I was afraid."

EBONIE WHITE, HOW LONG DID IT TAKE FOR YOU
TO I.D. TYQUAN KNOX?
"About thirty seconds."

Cross-examination (Mr. Sweeney)

ALL THREE OF YOU WERE THERE AT RICKY'S PARTY,
AMBER, KHRISTINA, AND YOU, CORRECT?
"Yes, but we didn't talk to him."

Re-direct (D.A. Meyers)

YOU WERE NOT THERE WITH TYQUAN AT THE
PARTY, WERE YOU?
"No."

KHRISTINA AND AMBER WERE NOT WITH TYQUAN
AT THE PARTY, WERE THEY?
"No."

WITNESS #5, DAISY

Daisy talked about spending the night with her grandmother, Pamala
Lark. On January 4, 2007, she and Pam left the house to pick up

a from school. After Pam went to the garbage bin to throw some trash, a man with a gun came out of nowhere and asked Pam's purse while pointing a gun at her. Daisy was holding her two-year-old baby brother Gregory when Pam was shot. She stated she heard four gunshots, saw her grandmother fall to the ground with blood coming from her body, with no sign of life in her body, still holding her purse.

She talked about how her grandmother kept the gunman's attention directed at her, protecting her grandchildren from his notice although they were standing three feet away.

It was as if they were invisible to him. She saw a man about six feet tall dressed all in black with only his eyes visible. She said they were Tyquan's eyes.

WHO DID YOU CALL AFTER THE SHOOTING?
"I called my Uncle Michael and tried to call 911, but the line was busy. He said he was on his way."

Daisy is shown a diagram of the apartment next door and asked if she saw anyone in that area. She said no.

Cross-examination (Ms. Powell)

WHERE DID THE MAN COME FROM?
"I don't know."

WHERE WERE YOU?
Daisy showed the defense on the diagram that she was standing approximately three feet away from the gunman. Pam's car was backed into the parking stall, and they (Daisy and Pam) were on the driver's side, getting ready to put Gregory in the car seat behind the driver's seat.

HOW MUCH TIME DID YOU SPEND LOOKING AT THE GUNMAN?
"I looked at him from about thirty seconds to one minute. I alternated looking at him and my grandmother."

(About 80 percent of the time she was focused on the gunman.)

CAN YOU DESCRIBE THE EYES OF THE GUNMAN FOR US?
"I can't. I just know they were menacing."

WHAT SHAPE ARE HIS EYES?
"I don't know how to do that. I just know by looking at him in person. You never forget a traumatic event like that."

CAN YOU DESCRIBE THE PANTS?
"No, I just know they were all black."

DESCRIBE THE DEFENDANT'S EYES WITHOUT LOOKING AT HIM.
"I can't; I can only describe how I feel when I look into them."

Re-direct (D.A. Meyers)

HOW TALL WAS THE DEFENDANT?
"About six feet tall."

WAS ANYTHING TAKEN FROM YOU?
"No."

DID THE MAN TOUCH THE CAR?
"No."

DID HE HAVE ON GLOVES?
"Yes."

HOW MANY TIMES DID YOU CALL 911?
"Twice I got a busy signal."

WITNESS #6, MARIO VILLIABOS

Mario told his story of how he was lying in bed watching TV. (He lived at 2233 Marvin Avenue, across from Pam's apartment and driveway.) He heard four gunshots and then his cousin Flor came running downstairs from her apartment stating that someone got shot.

His apartment was in the front of the building. He was quickly checking his family to see if anyone was hurt when he saw a man with a dark sweater on try and open the gate that connected his and Pam's driveway.

He watched the man go to the front of his apartment and try to open his front gate, which was locked. Then he jumped the fence.

HOW TALL WAS THE MAN?
"About my height or taller. I'm 5'8"."

WHAT COLOR IN COMPLEXION WAS THE PERSON?
"He was a light-skinned black person."

DID YOU SEE THE PERSON'S FACE?
"No."

WHAT DIRECTION DID THE PERSON RUN?
"North, towards Washington."

DID YOU SEE THE PERSON WHO WAS SHOT?
"Yes, I saw my neighbor lying on the ground."

DID YOU TOUCH HER?
"No, I stayed about a hundred feet away from her."

Cross-examination (Ms. Powell)

YOU SAID YOUR COUSIN FLOR RAN DOWN STAIRS SCREAMING. DID SHE GO OUTSIDE?
"No, she was scared."

DID YOU TELL THE POLICE YOUR COUSIN FLOR SAW THE GUNMAN HOP THE FENCE?
"No, I was translating for her. I don't know what she saw."

WHAT IS THE DISTANCE TO THE DRIVEWAY?
"I don't know; I'm not good at measuring in feet."

WHEN DID YOU SEE THE PERSON'S FACE?
"I never saw his face. I saw his wrist when he tried to open the gate."

DID YOU SEE HIS HANDS?
"No."

CAN YOU POINT OUT SOMEONE WITH HIS SKIN COLOR?
(MARIO POINTS TO MS. POWELL.)

SO YOU ONLY SAW ABOUT 1 PERCENT OF SKIN AND DETERMINED HE HAD MY SKIN COLOR BY THAT?
"Yes."

DID YOU NOTICE ANY TATTOOS ON THE WRIST?
"No."

The defense attorneys showed that Tyquan has tattoos on both his forearms. This was not the 1 percent of skin Mario saw. They pointed out he said he saw a gunman running towards Washington at the same time he was on the phone to 911. He was shown a police report to refresh his memory. Mario said that this was not his statement; it was him translating for his cousin Flor.

TODAY IN COURT IS THIS THE FIRST TIME YOU HAVE GIVEN A STATEMENT ABOUT THE GUNMAN BEING 5'8" OR TALLER AND HIS SKIN COLOR?
"This is the first time I remember giving a description of the suspect."

WITNESS #7, JAMIE MELGAR

(Spanish speaker—interpreter used)

He talked about what happened on 1-4-07 while he was sitting in his car eating at around 0900 hours. He was across the street from the gunshots, on Marvin. After the shots were fired, he saw a person hop a fence dressed in black, walking very fast then running toward Washington. He said the face was covered with a bandana or pantyhose type of material. The person was around six feet fall. He saw the person hop the fence very easily. He was unsure if the person was a man or woman. He said it took about ten or eleven seconds for the person to get to Washington. Then he proceeded east.

Cross examination (Mr. Sweeney)

WHAT WAS THE DISTANCE TO WASHINGTON?
"I don't know."

WHAT TIME DID YOU TALK TO THE POLICE?
"Around 0900 hours."

DID YOU GO TO THE POLICE STATION?
"I don't recall."

DID YOU GIVE A STATEMENT TO THE POLICE ABOUT AN HOUR AFTER THE SHOOTING?
"I don't recall, maybe about an hour."

DID THEY ASK FOR A DESCRIPTION OF THE SUSPECT?
"I don't recall. I just told them he was tall."

DID YOU SAY HE WAS 6'3" OR 6'4"?
"It was six feet more or less, bigger than me."

DID YOU SAY 6'4"?

"I believe so, more or less."

DID YOU POINT TO ANOTHER OFFICER IN THE ROOM AND SAY HE WAS THAT TALL?

"I said more or less as tall as you."

BREAK FOR THE DAY

CHAPTER 47

Re-direct (D.A. Meyers)

She asked him how tall he was. Witness said the killer was 1.5 meters tall. He said he doesn't know feet, only meters. He said he only knew the suspect was taller than him.

He said he does not remember saying the suspect was 6'4" but may have said it. The truth was he just didn't know.

Cross-examination (Mr. Sweeney)

YOU WERE INTERVIEWED WITHIN AN HOUR OF THE CRIME, CORRECT?
"I don't know."

DID YOU GIVE THE DESCRIPTION ON THE DAY OF THE CRIME?
"Yes."

He was asked for his driver's license and was told it said he was 5'5" tall and asked if he used the police officers in the room as reference.
"I don't recall. I just remember the day of the shooting, a man dressed all in black, running towards Washington. I will remember

that day for the rest of my life because for about a month I couldn't sleep."

DO YOU REMEMBER GIVING THE POLICE A REPORT OF THE HEIGHT OF 6'3" OR 6'4"?
"No, I don't."

WITNESS #8, DETECTIVE FRANK BOLAN

(Background: working the Wilshire Division, thirty-eight years on the L.A.P.D. His partner is Detective Cade).

ON 1-04-07 At 10:26 am, he received a reported shooting call. He did a walk-through of the crime sense and requested photos and prints to be taken. He identified seven pieces of evidence.
#1 A cellophane wrapper.
#2 Flip-flops of the victim
#3 Earrings of the victim.
#4 A receipt no the ground
#5 A baby bottle
#6 A pair of black sweat pants
#7 A doll

There were no bullets casings found and no gun.
On the electrical panel, he found a coffee cup and straw that he also broke into evidence. He said the investigating officers were Detectives Holguine and Urina.
He located two witnesses, Flor and Mario, and interviewed them.
He said they spoke poor English and the interview was difficult with no interpreters available (Mario speaks very good English). He said he tried to separate them, but Flor didn't speak English, and he needed Mario to interpret for him. This is not normal procedure for the L.A.P.D., but he was short-handed and made do. He said at first Mario said he didn't see anything, but his Cousin Flor did.

He said he got what he needed from Flor and did not interview Mario. He told the witnesses they would be contacted by someone else from the L.A.P.D.

DID YOU ASK MARIO IF HE SAW ANYTHING?
"They were both talking at the same time about what they saw."

DID YOU ASK HIM WHAT HE SAW?
"No."

DID YOU GET ANOTHER OFFICER TO GET AN ACCOUNT OF WHAT HAPPENED?
"Not me. Other officers may have."

DID YOU LEARN THE VICTIM HAD PASSED AWAY?
"Yes."

WAS THERE A BAKERY ON MARVIN AVE?
"Yes, and there were three cameras at the bakery. I obtained still photos on the same day of the investigation of the crime scene."

(The detective was shown eight pages of pictures of a man running down Marvin Avenue, northbound, dressed in black clothing. The time stamp on the bakery photos was 0930.)

DO YOU KNOW IF THE TIME ON THE PICTURES IS CORRECT?
"No, I don't."

Cross-examination (Mr. Sweeney)

WHAT TIME DID YOU ARRIVE ON SCENE?
"I'm not sure. Between 10:20-10:48 am. The call log said the 911 call came in at 9:55 am."

The detective was asked about his notes concerning the interview with Mario. He stated Mario spoke in broken English and was very nervous. He said Mario stated he heard four gunshots while he was watching TV.

IS IT YOUR RECOLLECTION MARIO WAS RELATING INFORMATION HE GOT FROM FLOR?
"Yes."

DID MARIO GIVE YOU A DESCRIPTION OF WHAT THE SUSPECT DID?
"Yes."

DID MARIO INDICATE TO YOU HE SAW A MAN IN BLACK CLOTHING?
"Yes, he did."

DID HE SAY HE SAW THE WRISTBAND OF THE SUSPECT?
"What!! No, he did not."

WOULD COLOR BE IMPORTANT TO YOU IF THE WITNESS NOTICED ANYTHING THAT WOULD INDICATE THAT?
"Yes, it would."

The defense again tried to show Tyquan's forearms, but the judge stopped them.)

Break for the afternoon.

The detective is shown the coffee cup and sleeve from a straw and asked if this was where he learned where the suspect came from. He said no, he was collecting all the visible clues he could. He was shown a picture of a shoe print and asked if it was a fresh print. He said he couldn't determine how old the print was, but he thought it was a blood print.)

DID YOU THINK IT WAS THE SUSPECT'S FOOTPRINT?
"It could have been the fire department, paramedics, or the peace officers on scene's footprint."

WHERE DID THE PRINT COME FROM?
"It was in the area of the bloody pants."

DETECTIVE BOLAN, DID YOU OBTAIN THE DEFENDANT'S SHOES?
"No, I did not, only the flip flops at the scene."

DID YOU TAKE THE PICTURE IN HOPES TO MATCH THEM WITH THE SUSPECT'S FOOTPRINT?
"It was close to the crime scene. I also took pictures of a lead slug from a revolver found at the crime scene."

Re-direct (D.A. Meyers)

DID YOU FEEL IT WAS AN ISSUE TALKING TO MARIO?
"Yes."

DID YOU TURN HIM OVER TO SOMEONE ELSE TO INTERVIEW?
"Yes, for a formal interview."

WHAT IS A BLOOD PRINT?
"It's when someone walks through blood."

WAS THIS A BLOOD PRINT?
"The pavement was dark. It appeared to be."

WAS IT A COMPLETE PRINT?
"No, a partial print, the front part of the shoe."

WHAT CALIBER WAS THE PROJECTILE?
"Medium caliber."

WHERE WAS IT?
"On top of the bloody pants."

DO YOU KNOW IF ANYONE ELSE INTERVIEWED MARIO OR FLOR?
"No, I do not."

WITNESS #9, JEFFREY GUTSTADT (CORONER)

His experience includes over 6,500 autopsies performed. He examined Pamala Lark's body on 1-10-07 and took pictures of his exam. The head diagram was shown first.

WHAT WAS THE CAUSE OF DEATH?
"Multiple gunshots wounds, five in total."

He showed pictures of Pam's body, starting with a picture of her ear. He said there was an entry wound but no exit. This was a non-fatal wound.

The second picture was the back of her head, low, toward the left occipital area. He said this was a fatal head wound, as the bullet entered her brain stem. The same picture showed her left shoulder wound, the scapular area, with no exit. This was a non-fatal wound.

Number three was a body, left-side wound to the torso and abdominal area.

Number four showed her left hand with her thumb almost amputated. He said the bullet traveled through her left hand and exited through her thumb.

HOW MANY BULLETS? DID YOU FIND INTACT?
"One medium caliber bullet. All the others were fragmented."

WHAT DID YOUR TOXICOLOGY REPORT SHOW?
"It showed a painkiller in her system called hydrocodone."

Cross-examination (Mr. Sweeney)

YOU ARE NOT SAYING WHO THE SHOOTER WAS, ARE YOU?
"No."

DID YOU FIND ANY POWDER BURNS ON THE VICTUM?
"No because the distance from the gun was more than one foot away."

Break for the day with a motion to strike evidence.)

Motion to strike: Tyquan's video statement after his arrest on 01-04-07.

The video shows Tyquan in a holding room with his feet upon the table, appearing cold and sleepy He was left alone in the room for about fifteen minutes, He is talking through the walls to his girlfriend in another holding cell. Both rooms were being videotaped. The video shows Detectives Holguine and Urina come into the room and start to read Tyquan his rights before asking him any questions.

He answered the questions concerning his rights with "yeah" and "uhhuh." The defense said that the tape shows Tyquan never gave up his rights and never agreed to waive his rights to an attorney being present because he never said the word "yes" to any of the detectives' questions.

In the taped conversations, Tyquan was asked where he was today. He said he was in the Valley at around 0900 hours with Michalyn Jones, a school counselor from his high school.

Detectives Holguine and Urina come into the room and start to read Tyquan his rights before asking him any questions.

He answered the questions concerning his rights with "yeah" and "uhhuh." The defense said that the tape shows Tyquan never gave up his rights and never agreed to waive his rights to an attorney being present because he never said the word "yes" to any of the detectives' questions.

In the taped conversations, Tyquan was asked where he was today. He said he was in the Valley at around 0900 hours with Michalyn Jones, a school counselor from his high school.

HOW DID YOU GET TO VALLEY?
"She called me and picked me up."

WHAT DID YOU DO IN THE VALLEY?
"I helped her around the house. She came and got me at around 0930 A.M. I was on
96th street and Normandy, at my friend Ken's house. We stopped at Carl's Jr. to
eat when we got to the Valley."

WHAT FWY. DID YOU TAKE, THE 405 FWY?
"Yeah."

IS SHE MARRIED? HOW DID YOU GET BACK?
"Yes. She drove me back, and we went to the mall."

DOES SHE DO THIS KIND OF THING FOR ALL THE STUDENTS... OR ARE YOU SPECIAL?
"For everyone."

WHAT MALL DID YOU GO TO?
"I don't know."

The detective picked up a cell phone. IS THIS YOUR PHONE?
"Yes."

WHEN SHE PICKED YOU UP, WAS ANYONE HOME?

"Yes, my mom. But she didn't pick me up from home."

BETWEEN 0900-1700 HOURS YOU WERE WITH HER?
"Yes."

The detectives talked about his car and asked: WHEN DID YOU BUY IT? HOW OFTEN DO YOU LET YOUR GIRLFRIEND DRIVE IT?
"A lot of people drive my cars. I have three cars."

NAME SOME OF THE PEOPLE YOU LET DRIVE YOUR CARS.
He named two friends. He said the gray Impala Chevy was the car he allows his girlfriend to drive sometimes. The detective went on to state that Tyquan's story was suspicious, and a jury would think so also.

The detective said, Tyquan has a history of robberies and rap sheet, where his girlfriend has a clean record. He then told Tyquan he was being booked for murder. Tyquan said they didn't have anything on him and he wanted a lawyer.

Mr. Sweeney asked Detective Holguine about his interview with Tyquan. Mr. Sweeney made a point of the fact that Tyquan was cold when he was being interviewed. He was asking for covers and was not given one. Sweeney's plea was that Tyquan was tired and sleepy and cold when he was read his rights and never really waived them.

DET. HOLGUINE, DID MR. KNOX SAY YES WHEN HE WAS ASKED IF HE KNEW HE HAD A RIGHT TO AN ATTORNEY?
"Yes."

WAS HIS REPLY "UHHUH"?
"Yes."

DID HE WAIVE AND GIVE UP THOSE RIGHTS?
"No. We asked him if he wanted to talk about what happened."

WAS IT COLD IN THE ROOM? DID HE ASK FOR A BLANKET?
"I was not cold. He asked me to turn up the covers."

WHAT TIME WAS THE INTERVIEW?
"0200, ON 1-5-07."

DID YOU OFFER HIM ANYTHING TO EAT?
"No, sir."

AFTER YOU READ TYQUAN HIS MIRANDA RIGHTS, YOU SAID, "YOU CAN TELL US WHAT HAPPENED."
YOU SAID, "ALL RIGHT WE HAVE TO GO THROUGH THIS THING."
TYQUAN SAID "UHHUH."
YOU SAID, "YOU KNOW YOU HAVE THE RIGHT TO GIVE UP THOSE RIGHTS."
WHERE DID YOU SAY, "SO DO YOU GIVE UP THOSE RIGHTS?"
TYQUAN SAID, "MAN, I TOLD YOU I DON'T KNOW WHAT'S GOING ON."
HE DIDN'T SAY, I DO, OR I DON'T GIVE UP THOSE RIGHTS.

(D.A. Meyers)

HE ADMITTED HE UNDERSTOOD HIS RIGHTS AND THEREFORE WAIVED HIS RIGHTS. HE LATER STATED HE WANTED AN ATTORNEY WHEN THE CONVERSATIONS BECAME UNCOMFORTABLE FOR HIM. THEREFORE, HE UNDERSTOOD HIS RIGHTS.

(Mr. Sweeney)

ALL QUESTIONS MUST BE ANSWERED IN THE AFFIRMATIVE. THE DETECTIVE DID NOT SAY, "DO YOU

GIVE UP THOSE RIGHTS?" HE SAID, "ARE WE GOOD TO TALK?"

Ruling from Judge Pastor

I HEARD THE DEFENDANT SAY "YEAH" AND "UHHUH" FOR THE RIGHT TO ATTORNEY.

A COURT-APPOINTED ATTORNEY, UHHUH. ALL AFFIRMATIVE ANSWERS. THE VIDEO WILL BE ENTERED INTO EVIDENCE WITHOUT THE STATEMENT ABOUT HIS PRIOR HISTORY OF ROBBERIES.

Judge Pastor asked if the defendant's mother, Mrs. Taylor-Knox, has a lawyer, due to Fifth Amendment issues. He asked if she had been charged.

(D.A. Meyers)

I WAS NOTIFIED THAT THE ACCOMPLICE HAS BEEN TO THE CRIME SCENE TWO TIMES... ONCE WITH A PERSON NAME JUSTIN AND ONCE WITH MR. KNOX.
(She wanted that entered into evidence.)

WITNESS #10, JAQUE SMITH

ON 1-4-07, Ms. Smith she was taking her daughter to school at approximately 0845. She was traveling west on Washington and made a right on Carmona when she noticed a car double parked on Carmona. She proceeded to the Jeffrey Foundation on Marvin and Washington where her daughter attends school. She described the car as a gray Impala with a woman in the driver's seat wearing a tank top and individual braids in her hair.

At approximately 0930, she saw a ninja (a person dressed all in black) coming from the south side of Marvin cross Washington, heading for the Impala. She stated she saw him trotting toward the car. She identified the driver of the car in a lineup as number five and wrote under the picture, "Looks like the driver. Slender face and complexion of the driver." She stated, "I'm almost positive it's her." She said, "The ninja was as tall as 5'7", a couple of inches taller than me." She stated this in the preliminary hearing as well. She couldn't tell if the ninja was a woman or man.

She did recognize the license plate; it was yellow and black, with "Finance Auto" on it.

Cross-examination (Ms. Powell.)

DO YOU RECALL IF YOU COULD SEE THE NINJA'S EYES?
"No, I couldn't."

COULD YOU TELL THE SKIN COLOR OF THE NINJA?
"No."

DID YOU SEE THE PERSON'S HANDS?
"No. He had on gloves."

DID YOU SEE HIS SHOES?
"Yes, he had on black shoes."

Re-direct (D. A. Meyer)

DID YOU SEE THE FRONT, BACK OR SIDE OF THE NINJA?
"All the above."

CHAPTER *48*

11-2-2009

Witness #11, Keeairra – accomplice/girlfriend

She faced Tyquan in court for the first time. He shook his head at her as if he couldn't believe she was doing this to him.

She started by admitting she and Tyquan had a relationship from 2006-2007.

She went to Crenshaw High School with him. Her G.P.A was 4.0. This earned her a scholarship to U.C.S.D.

She admitted she had a 2005 Ultima, which her parents gave her to transport herself back and forth from school. Her car was taken away from her because she chose to live with Tyquan.

Her parents didn't approve of the relationship.

She started school at U.C.S.D. 9-22-06 and moved in with Tyquan on approximately 9-26-06. She stated she was not at the bowling alley on the night of the robbery but knew about the incident. Keeairra took a plea bargain for voluntary manslaughter. While in jail, she got into a fight with a peace officer and had a charge of battery on a peace officer. This new charge would go away for her truthful testimony. When she was arrested, she said a person named Justin (aka Rampage) committed the crime.

D.A. Meyers

WHO IS JUSTIN?
"He is a friend of mine and Tyquan's."

HOW LONG HAVE YOU KNOWN JUSTIN?
"Two years from 2006."

IN SEPTEMBER OF 2006 DID YOU LEARN THE DEFENDANT WAS CHARGED WITH ROBBERY
"Yes, but it was in October."

DID YOU GO TO COURT AT THE AIRPORT COURTHOUSE?
"Yes, with Tyquan and his mom."

DID THE COURT DATE GET CONTINUED?
"Yes."

HOW DID YOU LEARN WHERE PAMALA LARK LIVED?
"By the police report, from the attorney at the airport courthouse."

WAS THERE A DISCUSSION BEFORE THE COURT DATE AT THE AIRPORT?
"No."

WHEN WAS THE FIRST TIME YOU AND MR. KNOX TALKED ABOUT KILLING WITNESSES?
"About three or four days after. Tyquan said Khristina could not get on the stand."

HOW MANY TIMES HAVE YOU SEEN KHRISTINA HENRY?
"Once at her job in late November or December. I was going to get a general description of her. I knew her by her name-tag. I didn't know she knew who I was."

HOW MUCH TIME ELAPSED BETWEEN THE TIME YOU SAW KHRISTINA HENRY AND CONSPIRED TO MURDER WITNESSES?

"Approximately two to three weeks."

WERE YOU THERE WHEN MS. KNOX CALLED KHRISTINA HENRY'S MOTHER?

"Yes, I gave her the phone number that was texted to me by Ryan Benton."

WERE YOU PRESENT DURING THE SECOND PHONE CALL?

"Yes, although I don't know who called whom. They were already on the phone when I came in."

THE THIRD PHONE CALL?

"Yes. Tyquan said he didn't rob Khristina Henry and pleaded his case."

DID YOU AND JUSTIN GO SOMEWHERE AFTER THE DISCUSSION ABOUT GETTING RID OF WITNESSES, AND HOW MUCH TIME ELAPSED?

"About two weeks later we went to Pamala Lark's house with the intention of hurting her."

WAS THERE A LARGE PURCHASE MADE AROUND THAT TIME?

"Yes, a car. (She is shown a picture of the Impala.)

WERE YOU WITH TYQUAN WHEN HE MADE THE CAR PURCHASE?

"Yes. And two weeks later I went with Justin to Pamala Lark's house with the intention of hurting Khristina. Justin said, 'We are going to take care of the problem.'"

DID YOU WONDER WHY JUSTIN WANTED TO GO TO THE LOCATION?

"I knew why, so we could murder her." (Khristina)

THE FIRST CONVERSATION YOU TWO HAD, WAS IT AT TYQUAN'S HOUSE AND WAS TYQUAN PRESENT?

"Yes. Justin called me on my phone and said, 'We will take care of the problem!' He was worried about the robbery. He said we'd take care of the problem (Kerraira and Justin). Khristina could not take the stand."

WHAT TIME DID YOU AND JUSTIN GO TO PAMALA LARK'S HOME?

"It was around 9:30 p.m. We drove to Marvin Ave. Justin got out of the car with a gun. Five minutes later, he came back saying he didn't know what he was looking for. We saw Khristina drive by while we were sitting in the car, but Justin seemed like he didn't want to do it."

WHEN WAS THE NEXT TIME YOU AND THE DEFENDANT PLOTTED TO KILL KHRISTINA HENRY?

(She didn't encourage or discourage him; neither did she tell Tyquan about the her and Justin's failed attempt while Tyquan was away on a scouting visit for college. A few days after Christmas, they talked again and agreed on the date of January 4, 2007. They agreed that Tyquan would kill her with a handgun.

They knew it would not be easy due to the security gate around the building. Anyone coming in had to be buzzed inside. This was the last conversation they had before the murder. She knew she was helping him to commit murder. She didn't want him to go to jail. She was willing to take someone's life in order to keep the love that she had with him.)

WHAT HAPPENED ON JANUARY 4, 2007?

"On January 4th I was living at home with my mother. She called me and woke me up at 5:30 in the morning to wake up my stepfather. That's when I called Tyquan to wake him up.

"Tyquan picked me up in the Impala at around 6 o'clock in the morning, dressed all in black." (She was dressed in jeans and a sweater with her hair braided in individual braids, with a scarf on, sitting in the passenger seat.)

"We changed seats on 80th and Van Ness. I then drove to Pamela Lark's house and parked about four blocks from the residence. Tyquan got out of the car at around 6:20 or 6:30 a.m., and I parked on the opposite direction of the street because the street was a dead end. Tyquan got out of the car with a handgun. He had on gloves and was dressed all in black, no mask. He intended to kill Khristina Henry.

"I waited three hours parked on the wrong side of the street. When I saw Tyquan running, I started up the car, made a left on Washington and Tyquan jumped inside the car."

DID YOU ASK ANY QUESTIONS? DID YOU CARE?
"No."

DO YOU CARE NOW?
"Yes."

YOU KNEW YOU WERE LOOKING AT LIFE... WITHOUT THE POSSIBILITY OF PAROLE?
"Yes. I don't want to spend the rest of my life in prison."

WHERE DID YOU GO AFTER TYQUAN GOT INTO THE CAR?
"We went to McDonald's. I drove until we got to the 110 and 10 Freeway, then Tyquan drove us to McDonald's and made me get out of the car.

DID YOU ASK HIM WHY HE WAS LEAVING YOU AT MCDONALD'S?
"No."

DID THE DEFENDANT GO INTO MCDONALD'S?
"No."

HOW LONG DID YOU SIT AT MCDONALD'S?

"About fifteen minutes. When he returned the first time, he was talking on the phone and refused to let me inside the car. (He had changed his clothes. He had on black basketball shorts and a gray t-shirt.) Then he left me again and came back about five minutes later."

DID YOU ASK HIM IF KHRISTINA HENRY OR PAMELA LARK WAS STILL ALIVE?

"No."

(She talked about how he dropped her off at home. She said Mrs. Jones was following behind him when he came back around 1:00 p.m to drop off the car, so she could get it washed and go to the mall around 5 o'clock. This is where she was arrested. She states she knew she was being arrested for murder. She was told she was being arrested for the murder of Pamala Lark.)

AFTER YOU WERE ARRESTED AND YOUR MOTHER AND FATHER CAME TO THE POLICE STATION, DID YOU TELL THE TRUTH?

"Yes. I lied the first time, but I eventually told them Tyquan had something to do with it."

AFTER YOU SPOKE TO YOUR PARENTS, DID YOU TELL THE POLICE OFFICERS THE TRUTH?

"I told them the half-truth. I told them I didn't have anything to do with it and that Justin had committed the murder because I didn't want to get into trouble."

IF YOU DON'T TELL THE TRUTH TODAY, YOU'RE STILL LOOKING AT LIFE WITHOUT POSSIBILITY OF PAROLE… TODAY IS THE FIRST TIME YOU EVER MENTIONED KNOWING ANYONE NAMED JUSTIN!

"Yes."

WHERE DOES HE LIVE? WHAT'S HIS LAST NAME? DOES JUSTIN PLAY FOOTBALL?

"I don't know."

(She talked about how she and Justin went to Pamala Lark's house to case the area two weeks prior and how she drove the car because no one else would do it.)

IS THERE ANYTHING YOU HAVEN'T TOLD US ABOUT THE DAY OF JANUARY 4, 2007?

"No."

DO YOU WANT THE DEFENDANT TO GO TO JAIL?

"No."

DID YOU WANT TO MARRY THE DEFENDANT BECAUSE HE WAS A FOOTBALL STAR?

"No."

Cross-examination by Attorney Sweeney

YOU TOLD THE POLICE OFFICERS WHEN YOU WERE ARRESTED THAT JUSTIN COMMITTED THIS CRIME, CORRECT?

"Yes."

YOU WROTE OUT A STATEMENT SAYING YOU MADE UP JUSTIN'S NAME AND THAT JUSTIN DOESN'T EXIST, CORRECT?

"Yes."

EVERY TIME YOU TALKED TO THE DISTRICT ATTORNEY AND POLICE, YOU SAID YOU WERE TELLING THE TRUTH, ISN'T THAT CORRECT?

"Yes."

YOUR DEAL IS NOT ABOUT GIVING UP JUSTIN; IT'S ABOUT TESTIFYING AGAINST TYQUAN, CORRECT?
"Yes."

THE DETECTIVES TOLD YOU THEY KNOW TYQUAN DID IT, DIDN'T THEY?
"Yes."

AFTER SEVENTEEN HOURS OF BEING IN CUSTODY, YOUR PARENTS WERE CALLED IN, CORRECT?
"Yes."

DID YOUR FATHER TELL YOU THE POLICE TOLD HIM THAT THEY KNEW IT WAS TYQUAN?
"Yes."

DID YOUR FATHER TELL YOU THEY WERE GOING TO PUT A NEEDLE IN YOUR ARM?
"No!"

YOU'RE AFRAID OF YOUR FATHER, AREN'T YOU?
"Yes."

HE BEAT YOU AND DREW BLOOD, DIDN'T HE?
"Yes, he didn't want me to see Tyquan anymore. That's when I went to live with Tyquan and Carla." (Tyquan's mother.)

YOU DON'T WANT TO GO TO JAIL FOR THE REST OF YOUR LIFE. YOU HAD A 4.0 GRADE POINT AVERAGE, A BRIGHT FUTURE; YOU'RE WORRIED ABOUT YOUR FUTURE, AREN'T YOU?
"Yes."

Noon break

Mr. Sweeney:

THOUGHT ABOUT NOT SEEING YOUR FAMILY?
"Yes."

THOUGHT ABOUT NOT HAVING BABIES, CORRECT?
"No, not really."

YOU WERE PREGNANT WITH TYQUAN'S BABY AT LEAST TWO TIMES, CORRECT?
"Yes."

YOU THOUGHT ABOUT RAPE IN PRISON, CORRECT?
"Yes."

YOU THOUGHT ABOUT ENDING IT ALL WHILE YOU WERE IN PRISON, CORRECT?
"Yes."

THIS DEAL WAS YOUR ONLY WAY OUT, CORRECT?
"Yes."

WHEN DID YOU AGREE TO CHANGE YOUR PLEA FROM NOT GUILTY TO GUILTY?
"In June."

IS YOUR DEAL BASED ON WHAT YOU SAY HERE TODAY?
"Yes."

IT'S A LOT EASIER TO DEAL WITH SEVEN YEARS IN PRISON INSTEAD OF LIFE WITHOUT POSSIBILITY OF PAROLE, ISN'T IT?
"Yes."

WITH TWO AND A HALF YEARS LEFT TO DO, YOU WOULD DO ANYTHING TO GET OUT OF PRISON, WOULDN'T YOU? YOU WOULD EVEN LIE TO GET OUT?

"No."

(Attorney Sweeney talked about how dishonest she was. He pointed out this wasn't the first time she'd lied. She was involved in check-cashing fraud and filing false police reports. She set up her own grandparents to have their car stolen. She even took Tyquan's A.C.T. test so he could get into college.

Sweeney painted her relationship with Tyquan. She met him when she was in the eleventh grade. She fell in love with his football status and dreamed of being his wife. Her family disapproved of their relationship when her father caught her in bed with Tyquan.

The result was her getting a beating from her father because she called the police after Tyquan was beaten up by four of her Crip uncles. Mr. Sweeney tried to describe her beating as brutal! But she described it as a busted lip.

At this point, she moved in with Tyquan and his mother, Carla. He talked about her parents repossessing her car when she moved in with Tyquan. This was why she had access to Tyquan's

car. He asked her if she bought Tyquan a Rolex chain with her financial aid and some diamonds stud earrings. She said yes to the chain and no to the earrings.

She is shown the picture of a gold chain and asked if it's the same one.

"It looks the same."

YOU'RE IN LOVE AND WANTED TO BE WITH TYQUAN, CORRECT?

"Yes."

YOU KNEW THE ROBBERY WOULD HURT HIS PROSPECTS, CORRECT?

"Yes."

IN YOUR LETTERS TO TYQUAN, AFTER YOU WERE ARRESTED, YOU SAID YOU WERE SORRY FOR GETTING HIM INTO THIS. IS THAT CORRECT?
"Yes."

ON MARCH 1, 2007, YOU WROTE A WHOLE LETTER TO TYQUAN KNOX STATING THAT YOU KNOW EVERYTHING IS YOUR FAULT. YOU'RE DEALING WITH THAT AND HOPE ONE DAY HE WILL FORGIVE YOU.

IN FEBRUARY 2007 YOU WROTE, "SORRY FOR EVERYTHING. I LET MY PARENTS GET THE BEST OF ME. WHEN THIS IS OVER, I HOPE YOU STILL WANT ME TO BE A PART OF YOUR LIFE. SORRY I MESSED UP. YOU ARE THE BEST THING IN MY LIFE, AND IF MY ACTIONS CAUSE ME TO LOSE YOU, THAT'S SOMETHING I'LL HAVE TO DEAL WITH." CORRECT?
"Yes."

AT SOME POINT YOU GOT ANGRY AND SENT HIM A LETTER THAT STATED, AND I QUOTE, "YOUR FEELINGS ARE NO LONGER MY CONCERN!" CORRECT?
"Yes."

In her letter, she told him that she would have the last laugh. She was angry because he told her he didn't want anything else to do with her. She stated, "It wouldn't matter if you were innocent, because they want it to be you and I do not give a freak." She wrote, "Remember you struck first. Have a nice life!")

Mr. Sweeney went on to point out this was not the first time she had lied on the witness stand. In November 2004, she went into civil court and testified about being a witness to something that happened when, in fact, she was not present to witness the offense. (This was an incident on the football field where Tyquan assaulted a cheerleader.) He painted her as an unreliable witness, a liar.

AFTER YOU WERE ARRESTED AT 5:30 P.M., HOW MUCH SLEEP DID YOU GET? DID YOU NAP BETWEEN INTERROGATIONS?

"About thirty minutes during the hours I was interrogated." (The interrogation lasting seventeen hours, involving five different detectives.)

DO YOU REMEMBER SOMEONE TELLING YOU THAT YOU WOULDN'T BE THE FIRST FEMALE TO GET LIFE IN PRISON FOR BEING THE GETAWAY DRIVER?

"Yes."

YOU SAID THE PERSON WHO COMMITTED THE CRIME WAS JUSTIN, RIGHT?

"Yes."

YOU WROTE OUT A STATEMENT, CORRECT?

"Yes."

The statement reads that she had Tyquan's car and she parked down the street from her house because she didn't want her mom to see it. It was around 10:45 p.m. on January 3, 2007.

She said she woke up at around 7:30 a.m on January 4, for a doctor's appointment. Justin flagged her down and asked for a ride. Since it was on her way to the doctor's office, she gave him a ride and waited for him to come back. After about twenty minutes of waiting, she saw him waving at her and picked him up. She described Justin as a black male, 6'3" tall, 250 pounds.

THEY TOLD YOU TO SAY IT WAS TYQUAN, AND THEY'D LET YOU GO?

"Yes."

YOU WERE TOLD THIS WAS A SPECIAL CIRCUMSTANCE CASE, CORRECT?

"Yes."

YOU JUST WANTED IT TO BE OVER, CORRECT?
"Yes."

YOU WERE TOLD A WITNESS IN A ROBBERY WAS MURDERED, CORRECT?
"Yes."

Mr. Sweeney talked about how her parents came to talk to her, and she wanted to go home. Her father talked to her for about fifteen minutes and told her he would get her out of this if she would just cooperate with him. Her father told her he knew it was Tyquan.

He pointed out that Keeiarra told the district attorney and the police officers that she never knew a Justin. She made him up. He pointed out that she wrote out a statement to the district attorney that said she would not lie anymore. He went on to state emphatically that Justin does exist!

DID YOU CALL TYQUAN ON THE CELL PHONE OR THE HOUSE PHONE?
"I don't know."

SO YOU CALLED TYQUAN'S CELL PHONE BECAUSE YOU DIDN'T WANT TO WAKE HIS MOTHER, CORRECT?
"I don't remember."

DID YOU CALL HIS CELL PHONE THAT MORNING?
"Yes."

DID YOU KNOW CALLS MADE FROM CELL PHONES CAN BE TRACKED?
"I don't know."

Sweeney showed, using phone records, that there were no calls from Keeairra to Tyquan's cell phone. Keeairra said she didn't know how she called him. She didn't see him with a gun on the day of the murder.

YOU TOOK A DEAL IN NOVEMBER 2008 BECAUSE YOU DIDN'T WANT TO BE IN JAIL ANY LONGER, ISN'T THAT CORRECT?
"Yes."

YOU WERE GIVEN A DEAL TO COMPLY; YOU WERE TOLD YOU HAD TO BE COMPLETELY HONEST ABOUT WHAT HAPPENED ON JANUARY 4, 2007, CORRECT?
"Yes."

THEY ARE GOING TO EXAMINE YOU CLOSELY.
"Okay."

DO YOU RECALL WHAT MS. MEYERS TOLD YOU?
"No."

THEY TOLD YOU THAT IF YOU WERE TRUTHFUL AND HONEST, THEN YOU WOULD GET A DEAL, CORRECT?
"Yes."

YOU WERE WORKING ON YOUR DEAL BY BEING TRUTHFUL, CORRECT? IF YOU WEREN'T TRUTHFUL… THEY TOLD YOU TO BE TRUTHFUL AND HONEST, OR THEY WOULDN'T USE YOUR TESTIMONY, RIGHT?
"Yes."

THIS WAS YOUR ONE CHANCE TO GET YOUR DEAL, RIGHT?
"Yes."

IN SPITE OF THE FACT THAT YOU WERE WORKING ON YOUR DEAL AND TRYING TO GET OUT OF LIFE IN PRISON, YOU LIED, CORRECT?
"Yes."

YOU TOLD THEM A GENTLEMAN NAMED T.C. SENT YOU TO COFFEE BEAN. THE TRUTH IS YOU WENT ON YOUR OWN, CORRECT?

"Yes."

SO YOU WENT IN THERE TO INTIMIDATE HER, CORRECT?

"No, I wanted to go in unnoticed. That's why I brought a drink."

LET'S TALK ABOUT THE LAST STATEMENT YOU GAVE MS. MEYERS, IN MARCH 2009. WHY DID YOU GIVE ANOTHER ONE?

"So I could get my deal."

YES. YOU STATED THAT TODAY YOU'RE GOING TO BE TRUTHFUL SO YOU CAN GET YOUR DEAL, BUT DIDN'T YOU THINK IT WAS IMPORTANT TO TELL MS. MEYERS ABOUT PREVIOUS VISITS YOU AND JUSTIN HAD TO COMMIT MURDER?

"No."

YOU DROVE TYQUAN'S CAR WHILE HE WAS AWAY ON A RECRUITING VISIT IN IDAHO AND HE KNEW NOTHING ABOUT YOUR VISIT WITH JUSTIN, CORRECT?

"Yes."

YOU KNEW HE WAS FLYING TO IDAHO, CORRECT?

"Yes."

Mr. Sweeney went on to grill her about her seeing Tyquan's plane ticket the night she and Justin planned the murder. He talked about how she saw Justin with the gun (a semi-automatic) the night they planned the murder, and how she drove to pick Justin up, late one night, from 120th street and Normandy. She doesn't know Justin's last name, or how she called his cell phone or landline, not even how tall he is.

To make a long story short, we, my family and I, had to sit through three trials. We were disappointed in the jury's inability to see the truth. They were hung in the first two trials. Keeairra was no help in convicting the murderer; in the third trial, the prosecutor decided not to use her. We got the verdict we were seeking in the last one.

Praise to The LORD OUR RIGHTEOUSNESS! No weapon formed against us shall prosper!

Isaiah 54:"17

No weapon that is formed against thee shall prosper; and every tongue that shall rise against thee in judgment thou shalt condemn. This is the heritage of the servants of the LORD, and their righteousness is of me, saith the LORD."

Excerpt From: King James. "The Holy Bible - King James Version." Apple Books. https://itunes.apple.com/us/book/the-holy-bible-king-james-version/id557274051?mt=11

CHAPTER 49

Guilty

ON 7-18-20011 Tyquan was sentenced to life without the possibility of parole. This jury was able to look at the facts of the case and agree on four different charges. First-degree murder with a firearm was the one we were seeking.

He was also convicted of robbing Khristina and Donovan at the bowling alley.

Four long years after my sister's death, we received justice for the murder. Six long years after Pam's murder, the accomplice, the girlfriend, accepted a deal.

I was correct in thinking Pam's death would also kill my mother. Little did I know it would take away my father too (even though he lived in Ohio with his other family).

I felt like they left me all alone.

Not only was I lost without my mother and sister; our whole family was.

Depression was heavy in every house. I lived on tequila for a year. I ate, slept and worked. That was all I could do! We all gained weight due to the stress. It was a struggle to go out for any reason. Shonnie had a nervous breakdown and lost her job and newly built home.

Family members were fighting in different cities over trivial things. Family members were dying on both Michael's side and mine. We couldn't support each other like we used to… How could we? The flavor of our family was different, and we wanted all the ingredients we had before. We loved the taste of the different kinds of LOVE our family gave, the sweet and salty, bitter and tangy; now too much was missing at once.

We needed a break to adjust to the drastic changes.

CHAPTER 50

Board of Rights

The police department wanted to discipline Michael. They were angry due to the negative press they were receiving. The news media described the faults in the witness protection system. The *L. A. Times* reported our story from start to finish. They thought our story was worth reading for six years. They also covered Michael's board of rights hearing as the L.A.P.D. took steps to terminate his employment…

At Michael's board of rights hearing, I was given a chance to speak…

Hello, Gentlemen,

My name is Karen Lasley-Slider. I am Michael Slider's wife. I am also a firefighter-paramedic for the City of Los Angeles. I am a life-long resident of Los Angeles. It was my sister Pamala Lark who was killed on January the 4th, 2007. The reason we are here is because of poor police work and a flawed system when it comes to protecting witnesses. There is no reason why my sister should be dead. She did everything right. When her daughter was a victim of an armed robbery, my sister took her to the police station to report it. When her daughter started getting phone calls and visits from the robber's family and friends in an attempt to dissuade her from testifying, she reported it to the police detectives.

When my sister became afraid for her child's life, she asked for protection and tried to find a place to live. When her daughter became too afraid to continue with the prosecution of the defendant, my sister told her she had a duty to stand up to wrongdoers. From the very beginning of my niece being robbed, my husband had faith in his co-workers.

He thought that the job he would do as a police officer, his fellow officers would do as well. He told my family over and over, "The detectives have a heavy caseload. Give them time and they'll get back to you." When the detectives failed to call us back, he started keeping track of the detectives' progress in the case log in order to keep us informed. Throughout it all, Michael kept telling my sister, "Don't worry. They are going to take care of you."

When Pam was killed our whole life was turned upside down. We were so dependent on her; we were lost. She was the eldest, and she and I were the ones everyone looked to for guidance when things were wrong. We were a team—so much so that no one said our names without saying the other. Pam and Kay, Pam and Kay is what you would hear before any sentence.

She's been dead now for three years, and we are learning to live without her...but it's still so difficult. You see, we are a very close family. We get together often, and it's obvious she's missing.

Michael and I are now not only aunt and uncle to Pam's children, we have also become their parents. We have always been the kind of people others come to for help, and Michael has never turned anyone away. He is the protector and stable influence for those who have lost their way. I don't know how many people he has taken into our home and guided in the right direction. It does no good to count them... because every time one gets on his feet and moves out, someone else moves in.

I'm telling you all this because I want you to know my family looked to Michael for answers when Pam was killed. He cried out for answers from you, The Department, in so many ways before we arrived at this hearing. His focus was not on money or embarrassing the police department; he wanted answers. After all, without them how can we prevent this from happening to someone else?

As a little boy, Michael had one goal and that was to be one of the finest Los Angeles police officers. He was raised in Fresno, so his childhood wasn't tainted like mine was, growing up in South Central Los Angeles…I grew up watching teenagers getting beat up by the police. I grew up knowing there were places black people didn't go unless they wanted to get stopped by the police. Michael helped me to see a different side of police work. He made me understand police work was dangerous because officers are called to take care of the ugliness we as a people don't see every day. They are just doing a job, trying to get home to their own families after the job is done.

You are here to determine if my husband is a man who betrayed the department. I'm here to tell you the department betrayed him. Whether you accept the fact that something is very wrong in the way witnesses are being protected or not, the one thing you should understand is, Michael knows what needs to be done to protect witnesses, and every officer under his direction will know also. He has always been a good officer fulfilling the mission of the Los Angeles Police Department. He is an asset, not a liability. I know I sound very angry, hurt and upset, but I want you to understand, my sister, my best friend, was taken from me. Thank you for listening. I hope you will put yourself in his shoes when making your decision.

Still, they found him guilty on all counts. They said he wasn't remorseful, and they were not convinced he wouldn't do the same thing again. He was terminated after twenty-three years of service. Never mind he had character witnesses who stated he was an outstanding supervisor and employee.

They refused to make a difference and stand up for the witnesses under their protection. I was proud of Michael for standing up for justice. He was hoping to save other lives so Pam's wouldn't have been lost in vain.

So her death would make a difference.

My wonderful husband was devastated. He loved his career as a detective.

CHAPTER 51

Faith in God

GOD has a way of making crooked paths straight. Everything that looked like it was going to hurt us turned out for our good. Checks were coming in the mail so often, Michael would come in the house laughing out loud. It would always be just enough money for whatever we needed.

I knew GOD was working behind the scenes on our behalf. It happened so often whenever Michael came in after getting the mail, laughing, I would just say, "How much money did GOD send you now?"

Sometimes Michael would say, "He didn't send me anything, but he sent you something." I have never known anyone the IRS called to tell they had a check waiting for them from years ago.... This was after they froze our bank account thinking we owed them!

WE SERVE AN AWESOME GOD. NOTHING IS IMPOSSIBLE FOR GOD.

Michael and I felt like it was the two of us against the world. No one would listen to our cries for help, but the minute we stood up for what's right, we started getting hit from all sides. I can truly say we battle not against flesh and blood; this is a spiritual battle we face every day of our lives. Some of us just don't know it!

With each experience I face in life, I grow a little bit stronger. I see a little bit clearer and so will you if you live life with love in your heart. This battle is for our souls. It's for our lives! The dark side wants to separate us from GOD'S never-changing Love. THEY know who WE serve...

Psalms 83:18

That men may know that thou, whose name is Jehovah, art the most high over all the earth.

It's my faith in GOD that keeps me going no matter what Satan throws my way!

I see the future and it's bright. It's all in GOD'S Plan for us. He holds the Victory in All Things. Your FATHER has a plan... just be good. (Amen In Jesus Name)

Remember to love GOD First! Love HIM more than anything or anyone.

Second... Love your neighbor as you love yourself.

If you remember these two things and try to be good, everything will always work out in your favor. Jesus died for us. Don't take his life for granted.

Know the difference between who will die for you and those who lie and say they will!

This scripture called out to me on this day of June 11, 2015

ISAIAH 61:1-3

THE SPIRIT OF THE LORD IS UPON ME; BECAUSE THE LORD HATH ANOINTED ME TO PREACH GOOD TIDINGS UNTO THE MEEK; HE HAS SENT ME TO BIND UP THE BROKENHEARTED, TO PROCLAIM LIBERTY TO THE CAPTIVES, AND THE

OPENING OF THE PRISON TO THEM THAT ARE BOUND;

TO PROCLAIM THE ACCEPTABLE YEAR OF THE LORD, AND THE DAY OF VENGEANCE OF OUR GOD; TO COMFORT ALL THAT MOURN;

TO APPOINT UNTO THEM THAT MOURN IN ZION, TO GIVE UNTO THEM BEAUTY FOR ASHES, THE OIL OF JOY FOR MOURNING, THE GARMENT OF PRAISE FOR THE SPIRIT OF HEAVINESS; THAT THEY MIGHT BE CALLED TREES OF RIGHTEOUSNESS, THE PLANTING OF THE LORD, THAT HE MIGHT BE GLORIFIED.

CHAPTER 52

Xavier

I knew things were going to get better after my mother died, and a few months later, her seventeen-year-old grandson (Xavier) had a heart attack while practicing basketball drills.

Everything about that day was perfect for us to be in the position to encourage each other. It was the day before Thanksgiving. Linda (Xavier Jones's mother) and I were inside Costco, picking up the things we needed for Thanksgiving dinner. I drove to her house because it was her turn to host Thanksgiving. She was pushing the cart when her phone rang. I could tell something was wrong because she kept asking the same questions over and over again. I gathered enough information from the one-way conversation to know she was talking to the paramedics.

I put my hand out for the phone and gathered the information we needed to meet the rescue at the closest hospital where they were transferring Xavier. They said he collapsed while running down the basketball court. No one hit him; he just stopped in his tracks and went down hard. The coach and his assistant started CPR immediately. They used an app on the Apple iPhone. The coach had a strong urge the night before to download it and go through the complete steps of CPR. He felt the need to refresh his memory. What are the odds? GOD placed everyone in the right position to help.

—✺—

Linda drove. I don't know how but she did.

I ended up changing places with Linda when we arrived at the emergency room. The paramedics were restocking and cleaning the rig for the next run. I called out to ask if they had brought Xavier in. They said yes, and Linda jumped out of her car so the paramedics could take her inside to see him. After I parked the car, I approached the rescue, and the other paramedic introduced himself. This was the one whom I had spoken to on the phone. He gave me an update on Xavier's condition; it was poor. He was talking to me about organ donation. His description was of a person who had no chance of recovering. I started to pray and ask GOD to make everything turn out okay.

We had been through so much that all I wanted was good things, so I asked our HEAVENLY FATHER for NOTHING BUT GOOD THINGS FROM HERE ON. Every time a negative thought would tell me it was hopeless... I would rebuke it!

In the Mighty Name of JESUS!!!

I walked into the room and saw X on a respirator with two IV bags hanging and a crowd of doctors and nurses around him busy working on him; he was critical.

I had to mask my fear when Little Linda looked at me as I walked into the room. I smiled at her in reassurance and told her I was going to call her husband, Dwayne.

Xavier's coach was with Linda. I asked him to stay with her until I came back. Dwayne is an engineer for the railroad and getting in touch with him was too much for me to handle after the third busy signal. I called Michael and asked him to find Dwayne and tell him to call Linda or me. Michael did better than that!

He found and explained everything to Dwayne, picked him up and brought him to the hospital.

Family sticking together is a beautiful thing. Before I walked out of the waiting room, I was asked by at least two people if they could pray for us. I never turned down an offer. Everyone was praying for Xavier, not only those who knew him. His grandmother in Alabama had her prayer warriors bombarding GOD with pleas for help!!

We flooded the hospital with our love for X-man. His team-mates were waiting, crowded inside the waiting room. With our large family, it was too many people to count. Linda, Dwayne and I camped out in the hospital room, and his coach, Cooper, never left.

X-man was in an induced coma to allow his body to rest. GOD reassured us. Every time his pupils were checked, they were equal and reactive. His brain was responding, and we were hopeful for a full recovery. The doctors and nurses didn't believe us when we kept telling them Xavier was not on drugs.

All they saw when they looked at us was the family of a Black kid who played basketball and was going to get us all out of the ghetto. They thought we were banking on his basketball ability. They soon found out we were respected members of society. And X-man was and is just a really good kid. Just as we said.

We may have started out the poor relations of the family but not today. This is not what the doctors saw. Most of Ramona Jane Cunningham's children are in public service. Linda is a parole officer. Her husband works for the railroad. They own their own home and have a good retirement package for whenever they decide to call it quits. Xavier had a scholarship waiting for him at West Point. He hoped to become a pediatrician. He is the type of kid you hope your children will grow up to be. After the barrage of tests were completed, we learned Xavier had a large, muscular heart, and the electric impulses that cause his heart to beat were having a hard time stimulating the muscle to contract and pump the blood throughout his body due to the thickness. He needed a pacemaker. We surrounded his bed as he slept that first night in the hospital. His mom, Linda, Debbie (Linda's best friend since high school) and me. Debbie was stroking X-man's hair when all of a sudden she said, "He moved! Kay, Linda, X just moved."

I said, "Yeah, okay." I thought it might have been her imagination because we wanted him to move so badly! She started stroking his head again, and he jerked his head away as if to say, STOP!

She shouted, "See! He did it again!"

I called his name, and he opened his eyes. I started talking to him. I said, "You're okay. You just had an accident and woke up before we wanted you to. Squeeze my hand." He did immediately, strongly, so there was no doubt. I asked him to squeeze his mother's hand, the same result. By now the nurse was in the room asking X-man to do the same things he just did for us. We had to make sure he understood what was happening. And he made it clear to us he understood, and he was all right. No brain damage from lack of oxygen.

GOD is AMAZING! We started thanking HIM on the spot!

The nurse put X back to sleep. Finally we were able to take shifts by his bedside. After he opened his eyes and communicated with us, we knew he was on his way to a full recovery.

Although his brain was normal, his heart still needed fixing. Linda started asking around for the very best cardiac surgeon she could find. All inquiries kept coming back to the same doctor. The doctor X already had... The only problem with the doctor was, he had no experience in the latest technology in pacemakers. And nothing but the very best would do for our Xavier. I thank GOD He always puts the right people in our Lives. Our cousin R. Lynne King-Tolliver is one such person.

She is a corporate buyer who travels all over the world. Beautiful, of course—in our family, there's not an ugly one in the bunch. Thank GOD, Lynne just happened to have neighbors who specialize in both areas of the heart, the mechanical and electrical. She ran with them in the morning for exercise. Her neighbors were and knew the top professionals in the field of cardiology. After they realized Lynne was trying to help her little cousin, they told her they would provide the training for the doctor who was treating Xavier, as well as the pacemaker, free of charge!

Everything worked out for the good. GOD sent his earthly angels to rescue us.

Xavier went on to play basketball on a sports scholarship and is working on his degree. He is a walking miracle!

What if all these people who helped make it happen were not in sync? GOD knew what we needed before we did. He knew Lynne needed the friends who had knowledge and who would be there when she needed them the most. Xavier's coach was obedient to his spirit when GOD refreshed his memory about C.P.R. All things work together for those who love GOD, and GOD loves.

CHAPTER 53

David Jones

Our family had been getting hit so often with death and destruction, we were becoming numb to the pain! Our attitude was one of waiting for the next bad thing to drop on us. We started a saying to change our mindset. NOTHING BUT GOOD THINGS FROM HERE ON… (In Jesus name)

I reminded all of us whenever things got too heavy to handle. We repeated this until we believed it! This simple phrase changed everything!

It all comes down to FAITH! We have to believe it to receive it. It's just like when we were children, and we crossed our fingers to get out of trouble.

It never failed us!

My cousins and Pam and I were well into our teens before we stopped using this tool of FAITH.

As children, we used to say, "Quick! Cross your fingers!" (So we didn't get in trouble for something like missing curfew.) No second thoughts. Pam, Jewel (our aunt, our age), Debbie and I would keep them crossed until the danger had passed. I can't tell you how many times it saved us.

When we got caught and punished while using this technique, we always discovered that someone in the group had uncrossed their fingers. When we wondered why it didn't work, someone would confess they uncrossed their fingers for just a second! After this, we knew someone messed up if we got caught! The first thing we would say is,

"Who uncrossed their fingers?" Prayer is how I cross my fingers now! It is the most powerful tool we have. Use it!!!

Dwayne was the one who convinced me. I needed no more proof that GOD is real!His trouble started with a toothache. He went to the dentist and was treated with an antibiotic and given a temporary crown. He never went back for his permanent crown, nor did he take his medication as prescribed, and the infection started to spread. He started out feeling sick, flu-like symptoms. He refused to miss work, so he ignored the symptoms as long as he could, by taking over-the-counter medicine.

Linda went away for job training and was gone for a week. Her baby girl Brianna (X-man's twin) called Linda a few times to report her concern about Dwayne (her dad) being sick. She said all he was doing was sleeping on the downstairs couch. By the time Linda arrived home, Dwayne had lost approximately twenty-five pounds within one week. Linda walked into the house determined that he was going to the hospital immediately. This was June 27, 2014. Kaiser ran every kind of test to find out why Dwayne was so sick and losing weight at such a rapid rate.

They found out the infection from his tooth was spreading throughout his body. It started in his mouth and now it had spread to his heart and was destroying one of his cardiac arteries. He needed a heart valve replacement. But before they could repair his heart, they had to fix his teeth. A dentist came to the hospital and worked on his teeth right there in his bed. After a month of antibiotic therapy, they transferred him to another hospital for the heart valve replacement. It wasn't long after his transfer that his head started hurting. He constantly complained of a headache.

The hospital ran additional tests and found bleeding on his brain. The doctors thought the bleeding was from all the blood thinners he was being treated with during his twenty days of staying in the hospital. No one thought to test and see if the infection had spread to his brain. The hospital sent him home to finish his antibiotic therapy. They were waiting for the infection to clear up before they replaced his heart valve. He continued to have headaches for ten more days before Linda took him back to the emergency room.

By now he was lethargic and confused, unable to follow simple commands. Tests revealed the infection had now spread to his brain. Now he had two major organs that were being ravaged by infection, and his prognosis was poor.

He was transferred to Kaiser Fontana to address the brain issue. Linda and I were praying for our GOD and FATHER to intervene and make everything turn out right. We had lost so many people to death that every time someone else died, we felt a little more lost. Our little ones were going to miss out on meeting some wonderful people. Dwayne was confused and fighting us the whole time! Linda's voice was the only comfort he responded to with positive results.

All she had to do was talk to him, and a calm would fall over him for a few minutes. I'm not going to go into detail about that first forty-eight hours, but I will tell you this... GOD is Amazing!

GOD showed up and removed Dwayne from the hospital that was willing to just let him die. GOD heard our prayers and healed Dwayne right before our eyes. We needed no more demonstrations of GOD'S POWER. We know JEHOVAH GOD IS REAL. We, Linda and I, proclaimed it!

We stated to GOD we were ready to go to the next level. HE no longer had to prove his love to us; we see HIM working! We learned how real GOD is through our FAITH in HIM to deliver us from all oppression and evil, the oppression we see and that which is unseen.

Ephesians 2:8-10

> *For by grace are ye saved through faith; and that not of yourselves: it is the gift of God; Not of works, lest any man should boast. For we are his workmanship, created in Christ Jesus unto good works, which God hath before ordained that we should walk in them.*

I could go on and on about how GOD saved us. I pray that this book becomes a never-ending story about our family. I pray each generation picks up where I left off and declare GOD'S LOVE in their lives and how real HE is. I hope Daisy and Aunt Linda write their stories and so on, and so on.

Let us hear the conclusion of the whole matter: Fear God and keep his commandments: for this is the whole duty of man.

> *For God shall bring every work into judgment, with every secret thing, whether it be good, or whether it be evil.*
> (Ecclesiastes 12: 13-14)

TO THE SEED OF DAVID, FOREVER...
01-13-2016
My life story. And yours...

It just hit me! I am supposed to write until... My life goes on, so my story does also. I am no longer on the prayer line... I miss the ladies praying and joining in with their request to God. I know everything happens for a reason, and I know Jehovah is leading me in another direction. I was too vocal about what God was telling me to relate to everyone on the line. Some heard me, and some did not... God has a plan, and I'm on His side.

I pray for the prayer line every day. I think of them, usually at around 0600. I know they feel the same way I do concerning the words of David in Psalms 118:1-29. It all comes back to our Heavenly Father.

Psalms 118:28-29 reads, You are my God, and I will praise you; you are my God, I will exalt you. Give thanks to Jehovah, for he is good; His loyal love endures forever.

I may be a little slow in getting the message God is sending me, but I always get there!

On Monday, I was on Facebook and Fee had just done a personality test. It was to find her chosen profession. I clicked on the test and without even taking it, this pops up for me...

> Karen Lasley-Slider
> You're an authentic
> Author (IN RED)

It read:

You are blessed with creativity and are full of ideas. Above all, you want to create something beautiful that can make others happy. You have an almost scary ability to create masterpieces out of sheer nothing.

I also feel as if everyone is starting to live the good life again. This morning I was outside just as the sun rose to display the most beautiful shades of pink and blue. I saw a face in the complete state of peace. God is with us. I'm living again. I'm living the best life I have to live NOW! The Kingdom of God is inside me… I am under his protection and life is good. I'm looking for nothing but good things from here on. No worries. I see my God is in control and it all works out for those who love God and are called according to his propose.

Isaiah 54:

SING, O barren, thou that didst not bear; break forth into singing, and cry aloud, thou that didst not travail with child: for more are the children of the desolate than the children of the married wife, saith the LORD.

2) Enlarge the place of thy tent, and let them stretch forth the curtains of thine habitations: spare not, lengthen thy cords, and strengthen thy stakes;

3) For thou shalt break forth on the right hand and on the left; and thy seed shall inherit the Gentiles, and make the desolate cities to be inhabited.

4) Fear not; for thou shalt not be ashamed: neither be thou confounded; for thou shalt not be put to shame: for thou shalt forget the shame of thy youth, and shalt not remember the reproach of thy widowhood any more.

5) For thy Maker is thine husband; the LORD of hosts is his name; and thy Redeemer the Holy One of Israel; The God of the whole earth shall he be called.

6) For the LORD hath called thee as a woman forsaken and grieved in spirit, and a wife of youth, when thou wast refused, saith thy God.

7) For a small moment have I forsaken thee; but with great mercies will I gather thee.

8) In a little wrath I hid my face from thee for a moment; but with everlasting kindness will I have mercy on thee, saith the LORD [...]"

9) For this is as the waters of Noah unto me: for as I have sworn that the waters of Noah should no more go over the earth; so have I sworn that I would not be wroth with thee, nor rebuke thee.

10) For the mountains shall depart, and the hills be removed; but my kindness shall not depart from thee, neither shall the covenant of my peace be removed, saith the LORD that hath mercy on thee.

11) O thou afflicted, tossed with tempest, and not comforted, behold, I will lay thy stones with fair colors, and lay thy foundations with sapphires.

12) And I will make thy windows of agates, and thy gates of carbuncles, and all thy borders of pleasant stones.

13) And all thy children shall be taught of the LORD; and great shall be the peace of thy children.

14) In righteousness shalt thou be established: thou shalt be far from oppression; for thou shalt not fear: and from terror; for it shall not come near thee.

15) Behold, they shall surely gather together, but not by me: whosoever shall gather together against thee shall fall for thy sake.

16) Behold, I have created the smith that bloweth the coals in the fire, and that bringeth forth an instrument for his work; and I have created the waster to destroy.

17) No weapon that is formed against thee shall prosper; and every tongue that shall rise against thee in judgment thou shalt condemn. This is the heritage of the servants of the LORD, and their righteousness is of me, saith the LORD.

Jeremiah 29:11 (this is the message my sister Pamala Sue Lark left for us to understand... found on her refrigerator.) It reads...

11) For I know the thoughts that I think toward you, saith the LORD, thoughts of peace, and not of evil, to give you an expected end.

We no longer walk under the bondage of the law…. His law is written on our hearts, and we know he loves us, just the way we are. We walk in freedom.

I'm in the T.V. room listening to one of my LPs, a vinyl record of a musical titled *Purlie*. It's a play about Black and white relations at the beginning of freedom from slavery. This story has a lot of ups and downs, but it all comes down to the ending, which states—

"THE WORLD IS COMING TO A START."

This is how I feel today. This is the beginning of a whole new way of living. I embrace each day, eager to open the gift God has waiting for me.

Today it was a beautiful picture of the sunrise. A picture that is both fleeting and a once in lifetime moment.

21 Revelation verse 1-3

AND I saw a new heaven and a new earth: for the first heaven and the first earth were passed away; and there was no more sea.

And I John saw the holy city, new Jerusalem, coming down from God out of heaven, prepared as a bride adorned for her husband.

And I heard a great voice out of heaven saying, Behold, the tabernacle of God is with men, and he will dwell with them, and they shall be his people, and God himself shall be with them, and be their God.